Sulayman Al Bassam

UR

OBERON BOOKS
LONDON

WWW.OBERONBOOKS.COM

First published in 2018 by Oberon Books Ltd
521 Caledonian Road, London N7 9RH
Tel: +44 (0) 20 7607 3637 / Fax: +44 (0) 20 7607 3629
e-mail: info@oberonbooks.com
www.oberonbooks.com

A catalogue record for this book is available from the British Library.

PB ISBN: 9781786825650
E ISBN: 9781786825667

Cover image: British Museum/University Museum Expedition to Ur,
Iraq, 1926

eBook conversion by Lapiz Digital Services, India.

10 9 8 7 6 5 4 3 2 1

With thanks to:

Shaika Hussah Sabah Al Salem Al Sabah
Rasha Salti
Rima Mismar
Beatrice Andre Salvini
Oussama Rifahi
Martin Kusej
Brunhilde Biebuyck
Samuel Noah Kramer (RIP)
Ruby Lowe

Contents

Introduction

For the longtime reader and watcher of Sulayman Al Bassam's theatre, *Ur* is a particular treat. Where has this restless and totally fearless playwright-director gone now? Is his new play an Arabic tragedy or a German musical? Is it a presentist allegory or a deeply researched historical drama? A choric funeral or a farce? A satire of colonial hubris or a paean to the transcultural power of Art? And how could it – how *dare* it – be all these things at once?

Since his award-winning *Al-Hamlet Summit* burst onto the international scene in 2002, Al Bassam has built a rich dramatic oeuvre on the 21st-century ruins of European empires and Arab hopes. His *Richard III: An Arab Tragedy* (2009) skewered America's pretensions in Iraq even as it brought the Arabic language to a Royal Shakespeare Company stage for the first time. Its sequel *The Speaker's Progress* (2011) wrapped up Al Bassam's Arab Shakespeare Trilogy with an ambiguous tale of censorship and escape. *Petrol Station* (2017), premiered at Washington DC's Kennedy Center, embodied the pathologies of an Arab Gulf principality in a sordid family inheritance struggle, with South Asian migrant workers as 'rude mechanicals' offering political commentary and comic relief. The musically accompanied monologue series *In the Eruptive Mode* (2016), starring the powerful Syrian actress Hala Omran (also part of the cast that created *Ur*), interrogated women's experiences of the Arab Uprisings and the rollercoaster of euphoria and dismay that followed. Wherever they have ranged, never have Al Bassam's works let holders of political power, Arab or Western, off the hook. Drawing in viewers curious about the Middle East and its 'cauldron of nightmares' (as a *Guardian* reviewer put it), he has honed his tools to flatter and flagellate these audiences by turn.

Aside from great-power Middle East politics, Al Bassam's plays have probed two other recurring fascinations: the limits of political art, and the apotheosis of the feminine. His original play

Kalila Wa Dimna (2006), a riff on the life and gruesome death of eighth-century fabulist Abdallah Ibn al-Muqaffa', dramatized the risks of telling doubled-edged stories to power. Could political performance work? Would the clever artist triumph or merely end up consuming himself? Five years and a wave of uprisings later, Al Bassam's *The Speaker's Progress* closed with a lady's maid turned revolutionary, beautiful and unbowed, signalling to restart the movement that a repressive regime had worked to crush. His French production of Saadallah Wannous' *Rituals of Signs and Transformations*, the first work by an Arab playwright ever staged at the Comédie-Française, further dwelled on the terrifying energies released by a woman's sexual rebellion and a patriarchy's revenge; during her martyrdom, his direction held the noblewoman-turned-prostitute Almassa (Julie Sicard) at center stage, static and Christlike, for the show's final 20 minutes.

Now at last the two political forces that have obsessed Al Bassam for over a decade – uncensorable Art on one hand, female sexual rebellion on the other – have merged into a single protagonist. In *Ur* we meet the goddess Nin-Gal, daughter of the wind god Enlil, wife of the moon god Nanna, queen of the city of Ur. She is part Wannous's Almassa, part Cleopatra – a regal and confused figure whose narcissism, wilfullness, and charisma are inseparable. Facing an invasion by the enemy Elamites, Nin-Gal renounces war and opts instead for love and literature. She takes a lover from Elam. Foreseeing the destruction of her city (and suffering under a cruel siege sent by her father, whose tactics echo those of Syrian dictator Bashar al-Assad), she disbands the military. Instead she gives orders to open the city gates, fire up the kilns, and torture the poets until they produce verses so fine the world will remember them forever. She is a dictator too, but one driven to a higher purpose:

> Let them say of Ur that it was a city that raised its walls to the sky, but kept its doors open, a city that did not fight with weapons but, instead, wrote poems of exquisite beauty and even when death lowered upon it, Ur raised its face to the sun, and impregnated into clay the horror

that devours it. … What I dictate to you is the purest form of love.

In a world ruled by the sword, Nin-Gal valorizes the phallus and the stylus. She is spoiled, naïve – and of course, ultimately vindicated by the status of ancient Mesopotamian literature and culture today. The *Lamentation for the Destruction of Ur*, recorded on clay tablets around 2000 BCE and reminiscent of the Bible's *Book of Lamentations* and Psalms, is one of the world's literary masterpieces. Here the play shows both sides of the pat humanistic idea that although the city is destroyed in life, it lives on in song. No coincidence there, but a leader's deliberate choice, and *Ur* shows this 'cultural resistance' in all its cruelty. 'You abuse Ur to build Nin-Gal's glory,' the queen's own lover confronts her.

Yet, like the Ancient Near Eastern archeological sites where it is set, Al Bassam's *Ur* is a many-layered thing. *The Lamentation for Ur* comes to us only because some western archaeologists dug it up. Historically, the *Lamentation* was found among tablets at the University of Pennsylvania's collection and partly translated in 1918. In Al Bassam's reimagining, some German archaeologists, in 1903, have become obsessed with digging up Mesopotamia. Their Kaiser wants showpiece riches, things like the glorious blue 6th-century-BCE Ishtar Gate that indeed now graces Berlin's Pergamon Museum (founded by Walter Andrae, one of Al Bassam's characters). But the archaeologists seek something deeper and darker: words. Anti-Semitic and Romantic, they search for a Babylonian literary heritage that could unseat the Hebrew Bible as the authentic wellspring of world monotheism, allowing them to invent a Christianity not indebted to Jewish ideas. They go to Iraq in search of their own origins, not of a cultural Other. (Even here the team's motivations are mixed; some simply want to loot the site.) The ensuing intra- and intercultural misunderstandings give the text its bawdy humor and historical irony, accentuated by intercut scenes of contemporary Islamic State fighters and futuristic Arab yuppies.

Developed at Munich's venerable Rezidenztheater as a co-production with Al Bassam's own SABAB Theater and the international nonprofit Arab Fund for Arts and Culture (AFAC), *Ur* actualizes the understanding and cooperation its characters could not. The cast mixed German and Arab actors; the script and rehearsals inhabited three languages. (In a nod to this interlingual movement, this book incorporates Arabic texts of the eleven scenes set in ancient Ur and a monologue by a contemporary Iraqi archaeologist assassinated by Islamic State fighters.) This polyphonic text invites a spectrum of Arabic and non-Arabic-speaking audiences. In Germany's changing theatrical landscape – enriched by the arrival of hundreds of thousands of Arabic speakers since 2015 and reshaped by the cultural elite's interest in Arab sources and refugee-related thematics – the Munich production is likely to find them.

Al Bassam is an incorrigible reviser, and one suspects this play, too, will continue to evolve. Nin-Gal's story and its frames would repay production outside Germany as well; there is more to say. For instance, Al Bassam quotes and thanks but does not dramatize the figure of Samuel Noah Kramer, the Ukrainian-born Jewish American Assyriologist who located much of the *Lamentation for Ur* in Istanbul. One wonders about his life as a Guggenheim fellow in Turkey from 1937 to 1940: did he meet Erich Auerbach and the other German Jewish refugees fleeing Hitler whose work would transform Euro-American humanities scholarship? As World War II broke out, did Kramer talk with them about the hard sunlight of the Ancient Near East and the poetry it inspired? Today, defending their country's decision to welcome Arab and Turkish refugees and exiles, German politicians often mention wartime Turkey's reception of these German Jewish scholars. To say that now the shoe is on the other foot is self-congratulatory but also true; the recent influx of Middle Eastern talent to Germany has been astonishing. Yet Germany is not alone in hosting a diaspora of talented, highly trained Middle Eastern artists and mixed Arabic-speaking audiences. A generation of Arab directors in many parts of

Europe and the United States is preparing to rise, and for these people Al Bassam's pioneering body of work has set the terms of engagement. The histories are likely to grow still more tangled, the polyphony still more complex. The rich and elusive text you hold in your hands is not an epilogue but a chapter in that story.

Margaret Litvin
Associate Professor of Arabic & Comparative Literature
Boston University

Dramatis Personae

SCENES FROM BABYLON, 1903 (THE D.O.G. DIG DING)

HERR ROBERT KOLDEWEY, Archeologist

HERR PROFESSOR FRIEDRICH DELITZCH, Philologist

HERR WALTER ANDRAE, Illustrator, Koldewey's assistant

HERR BELL, Photographer
(A woman, disguised as a man)

HAMMOUDI, Iraqi site Foreman

SABRIYA, a prostitute
(A man, disguised as a woman)

KHATOUN, a prostitute

BARA'A, a prostitute

SCENES FROM UR, 2004 B.C.

NANNA, God of the Moon and Deity of Ur,
Nin-Gal's husband

ENLIL, God of the Wind, Nin-Gal's Father

ENKI, God of Water, Nin-Gal's Uncle

NIN-GAL, Queen of Ur

ELAM, Nin-Gal's lover

PRIESTESS, High Priestess of Ur

DIYALA, Nin-Gal's attendant, a mute[1]

A BEETLE, the dream carrier

---

1   Diyala's lines are delivered through a corporal language.

SCENES FROM PALMYRA, 2015

KHALED AL ASAAD, Assyriologist (b.1932 – d.2015)

SOLDIER 1, Fighter for the Army of the Islamic State

SOLDIER 2, Fighter for the Army of the Islamic State

KAISER WILHELM II

SCENES FROM MOSUL, 2035

HUSBAND

WIFE

MUSEUM CURATOR

UR received its World Premiere at the Marstall Theatre of Rezidenztheater, Munich, on the 28th of September, 2018 with the following cast of Arab and German actors:

Marina Blanke	**HERR BELL**
	WIFE
Gunther Eckes	**FRIEDRICH DELITZCH**
	KHALED AL ASA'AD
Tim Werths	**ELAM**
	WALTER ANDRAE
Bijan Zamani	**ROBERT KOLDEWEY**
	HUSBAND
Lara Ailo	**NIN-GAL**
Dalia Naouss	**DIYALA**
Hala Omran	**PRIESTESS**
	MUSEUM CURATOR
Mohammed Al Rishi	**NANNA**
	ENLIL
	HAMOUDI

Directed by	Sulayman Al Bassam
Scenography	Eric Soyer
Lighting	Eric Soyer & Jean Gabriel Valot
Music & Sound	Tom Parkinson
Costumes	Carlos Soto
Dramaturge	Sebastian Huber
Production Consultant	Natasha Freedman
Props & Masks	Anne Marcq
Administrator	Saif Al Areef

The initial concept for this piece was proposed to the writer by Georgina Van Welie in 2009.

The production was co-produced by Residenztheater, Munich; The Arab Fund for Arts & Culture; SABAB Theatre.

The ten scenes set in 2004 B.C. were commissioned for performance by 'Le Festival des Ecrivains du Monde' at the Columbia Global Center, Paris, France, in September 2015.

This piece was inspired by the Sumerian text, *The Lamentation for the Destruction of Ur*. This artifact can be seen at the Louvre Museum in Paris. The text is inscribed on a rectangular clay tablet. In echo of this tablet, I suggest performing the play with the audience seated in traverse on two sides of a raised, rectangular performance platform.

The text has been written in English for bi-lingual performance in Arabic and German. The play can be performed in any language/s. Nevertheless, it must be understood that the German characters in the 1903 scenes speak a different language from the locals. This is crucial for the understanding of the colonial critique – and satire – presented in Act Three, scenes one and three.

The scenes from Ur, set in 2004 B.C. are a reflection on the events of the Syrian civil war (2011-2015).

RESIDENZ
THEATER

AFAC آفاق

مسرح سليمان البسام
SULAYMAN AL-BASSAM THEATRE

Act One

FRIEDRICH DELTIZCH's dream of the opening ceremony of the Deutsches Orient-Gesellschaft.

DELITZCH: Honoured Sirs, members of the Deutsche Orient-Gesellschaft. I present to you this map of Asia Minor and specifically the lands of Ancient Assyria and Mesopotamia. On these biblical lands, other great nations have established for themselves cantons of antique glory:

Persepolis, British.

Nimrud, British.

Ninevah; Khorsabad; French.

Borsippa and Ur, British.

Uruk and Larsa, British.

Kish; Telloh – the French.

Germany's inferior position needs no emphatics: a flaccid inertia, in sharpest contrast to our burgeoning intellectual achievements in the fields of Akkadian, Babylonian, and Sumerian philology. Yet to what end, you ask, the toil and trouble of Great Nations in these distant-dangerous lands? Why this ransacking to the depths of Arab rubbish heaps where neither silver nor gold awaits? The answer, sirs, to both questions resounds: the Bible, our Bible.

Yes, Gentlemen, for in the Babylonian dung heaps lie the true origins of our own religion: in Babylon, I say, not Israel; in Mesopotamia, I tell you, not the Old Testament! Science agrees with me, yet some continue to assert the moral superiority of Jewish monotheism over pagan polytheism, and why? The Ten Commandments? Hammurabi made them long before Moses. Noah's ark? 'Tis Gilgamesh!

19

Babylonian texts, lost for many millennia, now opened by our zealous eyes, reveal Moses' Pentateuch as little more than a jumbled assembly of inauthentic retellings and shoddy re-writes, these eyes unpick the signs, tap their mute forms and open their sealed lips, lift the veil, Gentlemen, lift the veil and see how the Evangelist granted to those Babylonian wise men – *not*, I tell you, *not* the self proclaiming, false, latter day prophets of the Israelites – to be the first to offer homage at the cradle of Christianity.

Miscomprehension of Mesopotamia: confusion in Christendom!

No small matter then – under the flaring nostrils of our Kaiser – this mission seeks to address and how it behooves the hand of German science to finger that dark mons of Babylon and revitalize the flesh of the Gospels that, as Goethe has already told you, 'glisten and gleam'.

No more wet than Goethe is truth and truth is Goethe and in so far as our science is our moustache -painted or real- no less determined than the Herculean Von Siemens who lays steely pylons day and night to forge the railway that links Baghdad to its bosom sister Berlin; so we too venture East with earnest zeal, fear and trembling to seek God and Truth! Pitching that German tent into the palm-crowned banks of Paradise, burrowing a tunnel through time itself, propelling the Babylonian wise men's semen deep into the flared nostrils of our father Wilhelm for Germany's tumescent glory: cuneiform orgasms, heaven-shaking thunder! Blitz the scrolls of Mount Sinai out of the virginal jaws of our twentieth century movie machine – no schmutz, no schmaltz, no kitsch, no kvatz, no Golem, no Moses, no schlock. German Will! German Christian will! Hot as iron, pure as blood.

ARCHEOLIGISTS' SONG:

To Babylon Now We Go
To Babylon Now We Go

Where The Earth Is Dark
And The Soil Is Wet
To Babylon Now We Go...

A Shovel Is A Shovel
And A Pick Is A Pick...
But What Lies Beneath
Ha Ha, Ha Ha...

O What Lies Beneath
Ha Ha, Ha Ha...

Is Nothing Less Than
A Conjuring Trick

Oh Oh Oh – Ah!

Oh Oh Oh – Ya!

This Stick – Who's Stick –
His Stick! My Stick!

This Stick This Stick
Of Know – Ledge
Will bray away
The sha-a-dows!

Exit ARCHEOLOGISTS.

SCENE 2: 2015

A stick of lit dynamite is thrown onto the empty stage. The fuse burns halfway and then extinguishes itself. Enter SOLDIER 1, picking up the extinguished stick.

SOLDIER 1: *(In colloquial Arabic.)* Not like that, not like that! How's that supposed to blow up a three thousand year old fucking pagan temple! Call yourself an explosives expert from fucking Germany! Come here, Einstein, let me put this stick up your arse!

SCENE 3: 1903

KOLDEWEY, ANDRAE, HAMMOUDI cataloging objects and fragments.

KOLDEWEY: Material?

ANDRAE: Inorganic remains, copper alloy.

KOLDEWEY: Type?

ANDRAE: Stylus?

KOLDEWEY: Writing implement: stylus. Location?

ANDRAE looks to HAMMOUDI.

HAMMOUDI: Jemb al chemindefer.

ANDRAE: Near the railway.

KOLDEWEY: Near the railway is an un-scientific designation.

HAMMOUDI: Jemb ma3bad Nin-Gal.

KOLDEWEY: Southern trench. Nin-Gal's temple.

KOLDEWEY: Period?

ANDRAE shows KOLDEWEY the stylus.

KOLDEWEY: Neo-Babylonian. What's the matter with you?

ANDRAE: There's something strangely I don't know what about a stylus, pressing its tip into wet clay.

KOLDEWEY: Cataloguing is about precision. Next.

ANDRAE: Clay tablet.

KOLDEWEY: Inorganic remains. Unfired clay tablet.

ANDRAE: With cuneiform inscriptions.

KOLDEWEY: Location?

ANDRAE: Nin-Gal's temple.

KOLDEWEY: Genre?

ANDRAE: Sorry?

KOLDEWEY: Accounts, legal or literary?

ANDRAE: *(Reading.)* Ga-s a-an-gal-men //
e-mu-ta e-kur ba-r a-ma-ma-de.[1]

KOLDEWEY: Literary. Late Sumerian.

ANDRAE: What does it mean?

KOLDEWEY: Its meaning is irrelevant to the catalogue.

ANDRAE: Please, I'd like to know.

KOLDEWEY: Nin-Gal... I... Nin-Gal... eyes... No: I see, I see house destroyed... I see *my* house destroyed... I see something house... Where my house... see a *strange* house... where was... I see a strange house where my house was.

ANDRAE: Nin-Gal broken.

KOLDEWEY: Put them in Delitzch's pile, keep him busy when he gets here.

---

1   Line 296, S. Kramer's transliteration 'Lamentation for the destruction of UR'.

ANDRAE: Nin-Gal displaced.

(Magnesium flash: the Photographer takes a photograph of Andrae holding the tablet.)

KOLDEWEY: Next, Walter. *(Hammoudi retrieves the fragment of the tablet from Andrae.)*

SCENE 4: 2004 B.C.

Sounds of a victory parade outside the darkened room.

NIN-GAL: I saw his ankles in chains… Calves strong as reed boats… Floating up the cage… His knees shine like helmets made of copper… His thighs rise like smoke from the cage…His hips are firm as riverbanks… His belly is like a camel's mane…His chest is a ploughed field – have you written?

DIYALA: I've written.

NIN-GAL: His balls are taut like young figs his sex like a road to a new city his arse pert as a leaping gazelle his back the shade of a cedar tree his shoulders are doors enameled in bronze his neck rises like a spooked heron his chin is like studded leather his lips are twine in new ropes and his wounds three I counted are all open.

DIYALA: This is a dark room, Nin-Gal.

NIN-GAL: It is not dark.

DIYALA: Let me open a window.

NIN-GAL: Do not open a window.

DIYALA: Listen to the crowds. Our men are back. Victory is ours. Your husband waits for you.

NIN-GAL: Sod your victory! Can you remember the description?

DIYALA: I can.

NIN-GAL: You'll find him in the prison.

DIYALA: This room is too dark, Nin-gal.

NIN-GAL: Repeat to him what I say.

DIYALA: What do you say?

NIN-GAL: Say to him: 'Elamite, prisoner of war. Nin-Gal, Queen of Ur says to you, "Your ankles were not made for chains, they were made to kick the air that's stacked like bad wood at the base of my bed."' *(DIYALA turns to exit, then hesitates.)*

NIN-GAL: I know exactly what I want. I want more than I can know.

SCENE 5: 1903

Day. In a trench. KOLDEWEY digging, HAMMOUDI, assisting.

PHOTOGRAPHER: *(Singing.)*
We want the old Emperor Wilhelm back
But the one with the beard, the long beard...[2]

(Time. Flies. Heat.)

PHOTOGRAPHER: *(Reciting the Arabic alphabet.)* Alif, baa, taa.

KOLDEWEY: *(To HAMMOUDI, in Arabic.)* Irja' – Step back.

PHOTOGRAPHER: Mud, bricks, flies and heat. Felix Arabia. Bloody wonderful.

KOLDEWEY: Small spade.

PHOTOGRAPHER: Exotic charm. *(In pidgin Arabic.)* Wayn ya Allah – where, Oh God – is exotic charm?

---

2   German Nationalist song, 'Wir wollen unseren alten Kaiser Wilhelm wiederhaben'.

KOLDEWEY: Trowel.

PHOTOGRAPHER: If only you knew the lengths I go to falsify my reports to the Kaiser. Biblical light, I tell of, dappling the ground between palm fronds and pomegranate leaves. Simple habits of man, I tell of, as if the locals had stepped out of Leviticus.

KOLDEWEY: Chisel.

PHOTOGRAPHER: And when I write to the Countess, to Fanny Von Reventlow?

KOLDEWEY: *(To HAMMOUDI, in Arabic.)* Look, Hammoudi.

PHOTOGRAPHER: I have to positively fabulate.

KOLDEWEY: The edges of the brick are beginning to speak.

HAMMOUDI: Bismillah.

PHOTOGRAPHER: The Countess is convinced I'm surrounded by hairless courtesans.

KOLDEWEY: Brush.

PHOTOGRAPHER: I blame Delacroix, blame David. Bloody French, obsessed with pussy.

KOLDEWEY: Air pump.

PHOTOGRAPHER: Must make you an introduction to that crowd, Koldewey; your simple upbringing, your ardent zeal, they'd find you quite the curio.

KOLDEWEY: Move this.

PHOTOGRAPHER: Hammoudi, you have the hips of an odalisque. Did I hear you say you have a sister? Ikh-tak? *(Your sister?)*

HAMMOUDI: Ikhtak inta! *(Your sister! i.e. Fuck your sister!)*

PHOTOGRAPHER: *(Reciting the alphabet.)* Geem-Ha-Kha. Wonder when the great master of Philology will get here. *(To HAMMOUDI.)* Wa-yn Delitzch? *(Where is Delitzch?)*

HAMMOUDI: *(In Arabic.)* On his way from Baghdad. Embassy said in the cable.

PHOTOGRAPHER: Zealous goat Delitzch! Decryptor of history, unveilor of ancient mysteries.

KOLDEWEY: Spatula.

PHOTOGRAPHER: Makes history sound like a strip show.

KOLDEWEY: It speaks!

PHOTOGRAPHER: *(To KOLDEWEY.)* You'd better find some tablets for Delitzsch to decipher.

KOLDEWEY: *(Calling)* Andrae! *(To HAMMOUDI.)* Ruh shoof Andrae – go find Andrae. *(HAMMOUDI exits.)*

PHOTOGRAPHER: Or at least a broken head.

KOLDEWEY: It's so moving. My hands are trembling.

PHOTOGRAPHER: It's not for smashed bricks, a lion eye here, a dragon's toe there that the Kaiser feeds you!

KOLDEWEY: Get up and do your job.

PHOTOGRAPHER: Precise man this Koldewey: Averse to alcohol, averse to women. Capable of great absurdity, this Koldewey. What am I looking at?

KOLDEWEY: The dots.

PHOTOGRAPHER: What dots?

KOLDEWEY: There are dots and stripes on this brick. It is a language of images that will lead us to the heart of the –

PHOTOGRAPHER: The puzzle!

KOLDEWEY: Just take the picture.

PHOTOGRAPHER: Berlin holds its breath in anticipation of Babylon's treasures. And here I stand focusing my lens on spots of a sun-dried brick that may lead to God. My God!

KOLDEWEY: Why are you learning Arabic, Herr Bell?

PHOTOGRAPHER: No good reason.

KOLDEWEY: It's a difficult language.

PHOTOGRAPHER: I'm of the opinion there will be war.

KOLDEWEY: When?

PHOTOGRAPHER: Perhaps not tomorrow. But, I'm a man who likes keeping my options open. Hold your breath! *(Takes photograph.)* Dots recorded for eternity.

KOLDEWEY: If you try to loot this site. I'll shoot you in the knee.

PHOTOGRAPHER: *(Reciting the alphabet.)* Dal-Thal-Ra.

Enter HAMMOUDI and ANDRAE.

KOLDEWEY: *(Tearful.)* Walter! Its meaning unfolds.

ANDRAE examines the brick.

ANDRAE: I experience the suffering and joy of light.[3]

KOLDEWEY: You were right.

ANDRAE: I feel my body fill with the radiance of colour.

KOLDEWEY: Yes.

ANDRAE: I see before me the endless, organic flourishing of the human soul before –

---

3   In this line and the following lines, Andrae is quoting from Goethe and Schiller.

KOLDEWEY: Yes.

ANDRAE: Before we lost God.

KOLDEWEY: *We* were right!

> *They embrace with tears of joy. Magnesium flash: the PHOTO-GRAPHER takes a photo of HAMMOUDI.*

Act Two

A soundtrack of wild and intense sexual pleasure plays at close range. The breathing of the two lovers is distorted into electronic feedback with reverb and echo. The intensity should be uncomfortable for an audience. The PRIESTESS sings with a supporting choir of voices. The musical treatment is operatic; lavish at times, minimalist and playful at others.

PRIESTESS: *(Sung.)* Nin-Gal, Queen of Ur, decrees the following:

Firstly; Ur, is an open city.

Secondly, Ur opens itself to any man: Sumerian, Obaid, Akkadian or Elamite who recites a poem worth inscribing, a song worthy of the lyre or invents a tool that reduces the burden of human labour.

Thirdly; Ur has seven doors, each door is an orifice of fecundity: erotic poems, are held in the highest esteem in Ur.

Fourthly: the women of Ur are freed from their bonds, free to share their bodies without fear of sanction.

Fifthly: Priests of the false temples, those who abuse the defenseless widow, tax the dead for burial and defile the orphan are to be imprisoned then banished forthwith, their income eliminated: Ur's taxes shall be paid to scribes not priests.

NANNA: Enough!

PRIESTESS: It's not finished.

NANNA: Won't listen to anymore!

PRIESTESS: Your wife –

NANNA: Don't call her that.

PRIESTESS: How would you like me to –

NANNA: Nin-Gal, Goddess of Reeds.

PRIESTESS: Nin-Gal, Goddess of Reeds, pronounces this decree. She calls it a vision.

NANNA: It is a massacre.

PRIESTESS: I read from one tablet amongst hundreds.

NANNA: Hundreds of little massacres.

PRIESTESS: Her scribes write day and night, her kilns are never cold.

NANNA: Break the kilns.

PRIESTESS: She buries them underground…

NANNA: Amputate the scribes' hands.

PRIESTESS: She's disbanded the army: in their barracks she lodges her scribes.

NANNA: I'm the God of this town!

PRIESTESS: Every night her messengers leave the city carrying her visions. Her laws, erotic poems and perverse ditties are being broadcast across the lands of Sumer.

NANNA: I am Nanna!

PRIESTESS: The people are besotted with her. In Ur, they pray to Nin-Gal, in Lagash they sing to Nin-Gal, in Akkad they make sculptures of her arse.

NANNA: Her arse! Her flat arse!

PRIESTESS: She dreams, she claims, through a beetle –

NANNA: A beetle?

PRIESTESS: A beetle with azure skins.

NANNA: Sack the whole damned city.

PRIESTESS: It took five hundred years to build.

NANNA: Write to her father, Enlil: Tell him to send in his troops, axes raised.

PRIESTESS: Attack his own daughter?

NANNA: She attacks him, attacks me, attacks all the Gods.

PRIESTESS: Set a precedent for civil war?

NANNA: This is civil war.

PRIESTESS: She communes with another.

NANNA: Communes?

PRIESTESS: Communes.

NANNA: What is co-mmunes?

PRIESTESS: Co-mmunes.

NANNA: Co-pulates. You mean she copulates: She fucks!

PRIESTESS: A General.

NANNA: A General?

PRIESTESS: A prisoner of war.

NANNA: A prisoner of war!

PRIESTESS: An Elamite.

NANNA: An Elamite! An Elamite free in Ur? A barbarian peacocking inside the walls of my city? Drinker of my people's blood, spitting cum on my palace tiles?

PRIESTESS: I tell you what is known.

NANNA: Bring her to me.

PRIESTESS: She won't see you.

Pause.

NANNA: You are a Priestess.

PRIESTESS: I am.

NANNA: You sing her visions, Priestess?

PRIESTESS: I do.

NANNA: Be her!

PRIESTESS: I am a Priestess!

NANNA: *(Threateningly.)* Be her!

The PRIESTESS assumes the persona of NIN-GAL.

NANNA: Nin-gal, you have cast off all sense of decency.

PRIESTESS: Your decency was a chain around my neck

NANNA: Have you no shame? You've turned Ur into the whorehouse of Sumer!

PRIESTESS: I create glory for Ur.

NANNA: By disbanding Ur's army delinquent queen?

PRIESTESS: Ur needs no army.

NANNA: Don't tell the Elamites!!

PRIESTESS: Scribes, pens, poems of ecstatic beauty; tablets, clay, kilns: that is Ur's army.

NANNA: Child-raping hordes, take note!

PRIESTESS: Its combinations are infinite, Ur's army is greater than any army.

Enter the ELAMITE, bloodstained.

He is the leader of my army. See his body: he sprouts in me…

NANNA: Heresy.

PRIESTESS: Vigorously he sprouts…

NANNA: Revolution.

PRIESTESS: Watering it…

NANNA: Filth.

PRIESTESS: It being lettuce![4]

NANNA: Enough! Into Nin-Gal's vulva, I will pour tar. Spit. Leave.

PRIESTESS, sobering, resuming her role as Priestess.

PRIESTESS: Nanna, God of Ur.

NANNA: Priestess.

PRIESTESS: I beg you to release me from the duty of singing Nin-Gal's visions: her beetle bears no divinity.

NANNA: You will continue to sing her visions. I want to know every detail.

SCENE 2: 2035

Mosul, Iraq. A luxury apartment on the thirty-fifth floor of a new building. A couple, perfectly appointed, admire the views. The HUSBAND carries a framed photograph by Ana Mendieta.

HUSBAND: Anyone would think…we were living…some kind of idyll.

---

4 'Vigorously he sprouted,' a Sumerian erotic poem. Jacobsen, Thorkild. *The Harps that Once…: Sumerian Poetry in Translation.* Yale University Press (1997).

WIFE: It's incredible.

HUSBAND: Look, we can see the whole of Mosul. Over there is the ziggurat of Ninevah.

WIFE: I remember seeing this town on TV when I was a girl. It was a completely destroyed city.

HUSBAND: Global capital. Magic. So. The Ana Mendieta photo.

WIFE: I love it!

HUSBAND: Here?

WIFE: Hmm.

HUSBAND: How about here?

WIFE: Higher? Off-centre? *(Shakes her head.)*

HUSBAND: Over here, then.

WIFE: Uhm.

HUSBAND: Hold it, will you, let me have a look?

She holds the photo.

HUSBAND: It looks amazing!

WIFE: Too close to the window.

HUSBAND: But the greens sprouting out of her body look so – wow! – against the skyline.

WIFE studies the photograph.

WIFE: She died like that you know?

HUSBAND: Who died?

WIFE: Ana Mendieta. In Manhattan. They were having an argument – her and her husband, I mean. She 'went out' the window of their apartment. They'd just moved in. Thirty-third floor.

HUSBAND: Oh my god!

WIFE: They were arguing over who was the better artist. Her husband told the police she committed suicide and they took his word for it. End of story. She was thirty-six years old.

HUSBAND: That's a terrible story.

WIFE: They were just married.

HUSBAND: Hey.

WIFE: Mmm?

HUSBAND: A: we are on the thirty-fifth floor and, B; our glass is a micro palladium alloy that can never be broken. OK?

WIFE: They didn't even have time to have a child.

Pause. Taking her in his arms.

HUSBAND: It's not allowed.

WIFE: I know.

HUSBAND: Let's find somewhere else for this.

SCENE 3: 1903

Day. Flies. Heat.

DELITZCH: You have an ardent passion for fragments, Herr Andrae.

ANDRAE: It is precisely through fragments that the ideal presents itself to the real.

DELITZCH: Schlegel.

ANDRAE: Herr Koldewey believes that fragments are more significant to our study than complete finds.

DELITZCH: And you?

ANDRAE: I am his disciple.

Enter KOLDEWEY.

DELITZCH: Ah, the man himself.

KOLDEWEY: Herr Delitzch, forgive me. One loses track of time –

DELITZCH: Herr Andrae has received me most excellently.

KOLDEWEY: ...when one is deep in a trench. We must show you Babylon.

DELITZCH: Of course.

KOLDEWEY: Many tablets await you.

DELITZCH: I lust for them!

KOLDEWEY: *(To ANDRAE.)* What were you doing?

ANDRAE: Professor Delitzch wanted to see my –

DELITZCH: Herr Andrae's drawings caught my eye.

KOLDEWEY: Out here in the tropics, you know, times overlap; none complete.

DELITZCH: *(To ANDRAE.)* And this you said was a...?

KOLDEWEY: Serpent dragon.

DELITZCH: Serpent?

KOLDEWEY: Dragon. Serpent Dragon.

DELITZCH: I'm intrigued how you came to draw such a thing?

ANDRAE: I relied on instinct and a process of deduction from fragments –

DELITZCH: How scientific!

ANDRAE: I –

DELITZCH: Yet odd.

KOLDEWEY: What is?

DELITZCH: I know of no word in Sumerian for dragon.

KOLDEWEY: He's not claiming there was such a word.

DELITZCH: Yet you propose the image of a serpent dragon?

ANDRAE: I –

KOLDEWEY: It is an image not a word.

DELITZCH: It is a model is it not?

ANDRAE: Yes.

DELITZCH: A model for the reconstitution of an artifact from fragments?

ANDRAE: It's only hypothetical.

DELITZCH: Artifacts!

ANDRAE: I could be wrong.

DELITZCH: Artifacts carry meanings that beg to be opened.

KOLDEWEY: Artifacts assert meanings that require no opening.

DELITZCH: Words alone penetrate meaning.

KOLDEWEY: The meaning we seek is foreign to words.

DELITZCH: 'Serpent-dragon' you say?

KOLDEWEY: *We* would see it as a serpent dragon.

DELITZCH: What would the *Sumerians* see it as?

KOLDEWEY: We can never know.

DELITZCH: I say there is no word in Sumerian or Akkadian for dragon.

KOLDEWEY: There is the Goddess, 'Tiamat'.

DELITZCH: Tiama: the glistening one; cognate of 'Tehom' meaning the abyss.

KOLDEWEY: There is 'Tam-tu'.

DELITZCH: The 'sea'?

KOLDEWEY: To ever assume we knew –

DELITZCH: I have read of scorpion men –

KOLDEWEY: What this symbol meant for the Sumerians –

DELITZCH: Monsters with poison instead of blood in their veins.

KOLDEWEY: This symbol of Godhead!

DELITZCH: I, Friedrich Delitzch!

KOLDEWEY: Of mystery!

DELITZCH: Tell you now there is no word for dragon!

KOLDEWEY: Is pure intellectual chauvinism!

Pause.

DELITZCH: Herr Koldewey.

KOLDEWEY: Herr Delitzcsh.

DELITZCH: Here at the Deutsches Orient Gesselschafte: we are a family, a community, always in harmony with the wider political context. The Kaiser is our patron.

KOLDEWEY: That makes me proud every morning.

DELITZCH: We will have no Creon and Antigone here.

KOLDEWEY: In the last year, we have revealed more of Babylon than all previous European missions have of any ancient city.

DELITZCH: Yet we've so little to show for this.

KOLDEWEY: Look around you.

DELITZCH: In Berlin, I mean.

KOLDEWEY: I cannot be reduced to treasure hunting.

DELITZCH: Indeed, we are agents of a much higher calling.

KOLDEWEY & ANDRAE: May God grant it be so.

DELITZCH nods.

KOLDEWEY: Allow me to show you the tablets I mentioned.

DELITZCH: *(To ANDRAE.)* To corrupt your friend Schelgel, 'The philologist is a prophet looking backwards!'[5]

ANDRAE: *(Bidding farewell.)* Herr Professor Delitzch.

DELITZCH: Show me the plaster cast and I will reveal the living flesh.

KOLDEWEY: There's a literary text amongst them, some sort of lamentation.

DELITZCH: I lust for it.

---

5   Schlegel, 'The historian is a prophet looking backwards.'

SCENE 4: 2004 B.C.

NIN-GAL and ELAM, alone.

ELAM: You cannot expect the people to hold.

NIN-GAL: Hold what?

ELAM: Your convictions.

NIN-GAL: My convictions are untenable: I hold them alone.

ELAM: Your stomach's not empty.

NIN-GAL: Sod stomachs! When did a stomach ever make glory? Look at mine! Sagging redundancy of flesh, made exquisite by the hands of my father's enemy. Lay your head here, Elamite.

ELAM: The Gods will turn against you.

NIN-GAL: Of course: I want a pantheon for man!

ELAM: They won't spare you.

NIN-GAL: I don't solicit their mercy.

ELAM: What do you solicit?

NIN-GAL: You! *(Hearing the chant of the PRIESTESS.)* Listen, it's being sung.

PRIESTESS: *(Entoning.)*
The wild ox has abandoned his stable,
His stable is abandoned to the wind.

ELAM: Last night's vision?

NIN-GAL: Yes. Sumer is sick, Elamite, a hollow vessel, a diseased body. Listen…

PRIESTESS: *(Entoning.)*
City whose name exists and nothing more.

City whose walls rise high to encircle only death.

NIN-GAL: You're shaking. It will all happen so fast.

ELAM: Leave, let's leave, take our love elsewhere.

NIN-GAL: What is our love – a sick child?

ELAM: There's no need for –

NIN-GAL: All need, all of it horrible, urgent need.

ELAM: I'll hide you in my mountains, you'll drink from the purest springs –

NIN-GAL: Don't be so bloody romantic!

ELAM: I'm a soldier, Nin-Gal.

NIN-GAL: A man of action!

ELAM: Let me arm the men of Ur; they're hungry to fight, to defend this city.

NIN-GAL: If I'd wanted war, do you think I'd have you in my bed?

ELAM: Then get to your father with my head in your hand and beg his forgiveness.

NIN-GAL: Fierce-eyed Elamite, have I turned you into a sacrificial goat?

ELAM: Go to him. His siege is killing the city. No medicine in the hospitals, no bread in the kilns, no fish in the nets.

NIN-GAL: It used to be in the villages around Ur, when farmer's children wanted to become scribes, their fathers would drag them to the village elders and the elders take a mallet, then pummel the child's hands till they were maimed. This way the Elders avoided the village losing a farmer. My own Father, Enlil, father of the Gods, liked this tradition; said it helped build communities, called it healthy and sent the villagers new mallets every year. Since I became Queen of Ur, farmer's children run to be scribes and their fathers help them run. The child's hand is in mine, it won't be for long, they'll rip it out by its roots, but as long as the child's hand is in mine, I'll help them write what can't be erased. What Ur writes will not be erased.

ELAM: My words are prayers, my –

NIN-GAL: Don't go on. I've made up my mind. I'll visit my father.

ELAM: I'll clear your route of corpses.

NIN-GAL: Undress me. Cover me with oil.
Ride my narrow boat.
Hard, you are the body of my resilience.
Limp, you are the body of my chosen death.

Act Three

Night, crickets, heat.

The PHOTOGRAPHER whistles: waits, whistles again. HAMMOUDI approaches silently, from behind. PHOTOGRAPHER whistles again. HAMMOUDI blows her hair. She jumps.

PHOTOGRAPHER: Must you do that!

HAMMOUDI laughs.

Be obedient!

HAMMOUDI: Labayk, labayk, khadimak bayn yadayk.[6] (Your wish is my command.)

PHOTOGRAPHER: Yalla. Shoof. Shoof. (Come on, show me.)

HAMMOUDI: *(Showing the stolen artifacts.)* Itfadal 3ini. (Here you are, luv.)

PHOTOGRAPHER: Good. A bull.

HAMMOUDI: *(In German.)* Good.

PHOTOGRAPHER: A tablet. Good.

HAMMOUDI: *(In German.)* Good.

PHOTOGRAPHER: A statue. Very good.

HAMMOUDI: Kullo good, inshallah. (All good, God willing.)

PHOTOGRAPHER: Hammoudi?

---

6   The Arabic is transcribed in Arabizi, an encoding system using Roman letters and Arabic numbers to transcribe Arabic, invented by Arab speakers for the use of online chat technologies without access to Arabic keyboards.

HAMMOUDI: Sidi. (Sir.)

PHOTOGRAPHER: How much can you fit under your dress without being seen?

HAMMOUDI: Ma fahamit. (I don't understand.)

PHOTOGRAPHER: I don't mean dress, I mean your your, you know, your dress – dja-lla-bah.

HAMMOUDI: Ma if-taha-mit. (I don't understand)

PHOTOGRAPHER: I need you to smuggle these off the dig. Not in a bag, on your person. Your body. Yes. Under your dress. All this. Out. For me.

HAMMOUDI: Ma fahamit. (I don't understand.)

PHOTOGRAPHER: Look, here *(gesticulates)* under here *(gesticulates)*, how much, how much can you smuggle. 'Kam' can you fit 'Kam'? (How much?)

HAMMOUDI: Ah, how much?!

PHOTOGRAPHER: Yes.

HAMMOUDI: Kam? *(In German.)* Wie Veil?

PHOTOGRAPHER: Smuggle, hide, yes.

HAMMOUDI: *(In German.)* Five hundred.

PHOTOGRAPHER: What?

HAMMOUDI: No less.

PHOTOGRAPHER: *(In German.)* Five hundred.

HAMMOUDI: Special discount.

PHOTOGRAPHER: Tablets, amulets, what? Five hundred what?

HAMMOUDI: Hatha babili, hatha sumeri, hatha akkadi, hatha 3a-mmi, hatha 7'-alli, hatha bin 3a-moomti, kulluhum ahil, wa dam, wa taree7'. Aqal min 7'ams imm-ya 7aramat 3alla arwa7i-him, ma asma7 li-nafsi. (This is Babylonian, this Sumerian, This Akkadian, This is my Uncle, This is my Aunt, These are my cousins, all my family, my blood, my history. Less than Five hundred is a stain upon their souls, I couldn't forgive myself.)

PHOTOGRAPHER: OK.

HAMMOUDI: OK?

PHOTOGRAPHER: Show me.

HAMMOUDI: *(Shaking his hand.)* Show me ana ba3ad. (Me too show me.)

PHOTOGRAPHER: Lift up your skirt, your dje-lla-bah and show me.

HAMMOUDI: Ma ifta-hamit. (I don't' understand.)

PHOTOGRAPHER: Dem-ons-trate. Show me. How much!

HAMMOUDI: Five hundred! Wa-illa 7'allas, ru7. (Otherwise, forget it, get lost.)

PHOTOGRAPHER: *(Becoming more demonstrative.)* I insist! What can you fit in your pants, round your legs, up your here – in your there – with your thing, do you und-er-stand me, little fellow?

HAMMOUDI: *(Appearing to understand.)* Ah.

PHOTOGRAPHER: *(Relieved.)* Ah.

HAMMOUDI: Yah… (Oh you…)

PHOTOGRAPHER: Yah!

HAMMOUDI: Manyu$! (Dirty fucker!)

PHOTOGRAPHER: Manyuch.

HAMMOUDI: *(Whistles)* Sabriya!

HAMMOUDI indicates to PHOTOGRAPHER to follow him.

SCENE 2: 2004 B.C.

In front of ENLIL's palace.

DIYALA: And now?

NIN-GAL: Worse than before, don't let go of my hand.

DIYALA: Two hours blind! Let me bring the doctor.

NIN-GAL: No doctor. The beetle can't make up his mind.

DIYALA: Pest.

NIN-GAL: Shut your mouth!

DIYALA: The palace walls are so cold, the doors so thick.

NIN-GAL: If I die let them say of me I built Ur's walls to the sky and kept its doors open, night and day.

DIYALA: You tempt fate. The Elamites are marauding across the hills, they hang children from spears and burn fisherman in cages, if it wasn't for your father's army that keep us wrapped under their siege, the barbarians would have swallowed Ur weeks ago.

NIN-GAL: You don't know the power of an open door.

DIYALA: They're coming out of the hall.

NIN-GAL: I can't see: describe what's there.

DIYALA: No.

NIN-GAL: Where've you gone?

DIYALA: I can't.

NIN-GAL: My eyes are swimming in colours and light.

DIYALA: What I see is too fatal to relate.

NIN-GAL: Describe it!

DIYALA: The Elamite horde – enemy to Sumer – and their
King – enemy to Sumer – carried aloft in your father's
chambers, adorned in lambs' fur his gems sparkling on
his bare breast. His followers are raising cups, singing and
cursing. Wine dripping like blood from their beards. The
Gods have received our enemies and their wishes have
been granted. It means evil. I fear the worst.

NIN-GAL: Blindness is a blessing. It's come!

(Seized by a vision.)

I am the bird that circles over the writhing city:
Ur, below, in hard grief churns.
The hand of the storm fingers the city like a glove
I scream, 'go back, storm to your desert,'
But its rib cage did not rise.

DIYALA: Your father is summoning you. Move.

SCENE 3: 1903

Enter HAMMOUDI and PHOTOGRAPHER.

HAMMOUDI: *(Whistles.)* Sabriya!

SABRIYA, KHATOUN, BARA'A emerge out of darkness in blonde wigs.

PHOTOGRAPHER: Who's this?

HAMMOUDI: 7'ti eins, 7'ti zwei, 7'ti drei. (My sister one, sister
two, sister three.)

PHOTOGRAPHER: Why are they all blonde?

HAMMOUDI: $iy-qool? (What'd he say?)

KHATOON: Yigool khawa-tik shuqr lay-sh, Hammoudi? (He says why are your sisters blonde, Hammoudi?)

BARA'A: Kull al Sumeryat blonde, baba, hi-chi ya-reed al Kaiser Allah ya-fata7-llah, wa yi-hafdha, wa yikhalleeh. (All Sumerian girls are blondes, baby. That's what the Kaiser wants – may Allah protect Him and Guard Him.)

KHATOON: *(In German.)* Your desire, stranger, breeds desire stranger.

PHOTOGRAPHER: You are exactly what I want to describe and can't: the other that I am not. *(To HAMMOUDI.)* Photo? I want to take a photo.

HAMMOUDI: Five hundred. *(To the prostitutes)* Yalla banat, Herr Bell yireed 9oor-a. (Make yourselves presentable, ladies, Herr Bell wants a photo.)

SABRIYA: Ani il bil kader bidoon jumal, bass hazz al tiz? (Am I the one in the frame who gets no lines, just wiggles her hips?)

HAMMOUDI: In-chubbi, wa hizzi tiy-zik. (Shut your mouth and wiggle your arse.)

SABRIYA: A-reed fi3il assasi! (I want significant action!)

HERR BELL begins composing the women for the photograph in the manner of early twentieth century orientalist erotic photography.

PHOTOGRAPHER: I must see you naked.

BARA'A: Ta-a-dab, ya wa7-sh! (Be-have yourself, beast)

SABRIYA: *(Sings.)*
Venus' birds, whose mournful tunes –

Sing lullaby, lu-lu-la lullaby to my unrest,
For so partaking of my wrongs,
In my bosom build your nest.
Lulla, lulla, lulla. Lulla[7]

KHATOON: *(In German)* Why is it that when you Europeans 'see' yourselves in us it's either a bomb or a dick heading our way?

PHOTOGRAPHER: *(To KHATOUN.)* Your German is most strange. Almost ancient.

KHATOON: *(In German.)* Is it not enough to break all a country's limbs and watch the body devour itself?

PHOTOGRAPHER: My Grandmother spoke in that lilt.

KHATOON: *(In German.)* Must you also fuck the corpses?

PHOTOGRAPHER: She met Goethe in Sesseneheim.

KHATOON: *(In German.)* Lace them in Uranium then in cum?

PHOTOGRAPHER: Together by the warm, wide Rhine.

KHATOON: *(In German.)* Herr Bell –

SABRIYA: Siktay Khatoon-o: Athay-ti-na! (Shut up, Khatoon, you're so ann-oying!)

KHATOON: Is Necrophilia an Official Religion in Europe?

PHOTOGRAPHER: Hold your breath! *(Takes photograph.)*

Following the explosion of the magnesium flash, the women start to dance wildly to the accompaniment of Iraqi drums. They systematically undress and pilfer HERR BELL who revels in a state of intoxication and abandon.

SABRIYA: Hatha moo wilid! (It's not a man!)

---

7   John Bennet, Venus' birds whose mournful tunes.

Music stops. HERR BELL scrambles to recover her clothes.

HAMMOUDI: *(Picking up HERR BELL's camera)* Minnik areed moo 7'ams-miya, areed 7'-amsat alaf! (I no longer want five hundred from you, you now owe me five thousand.)

Enter ANDRAE.

HAMMOUDI: Ja-nna al Wahhabi, injil-3an ya bannat. (The Wahhabi is here! Get out!)

HAMMOUDI and the GIRLS scatter.

The PHOTOGRAPHER, BELL, is left under ANDRAE's gaze. He pulls aside her remaining items of clothing and begins to sketch her naked body.

SCENE 4: 2004 B.C.

NIN-GAL: They stand still: I approach them. The water in the clock pours out time.

ENLIL: See me smiling at you, my beloved girl. Come closer: kiss my head, my sacred daughter.

NIN-GAL: Father, you have put Ur under a terrible siege.

ENLIL: Nothing of the sort, I have put Ur under my protection.

NIN-GAL: This is the third month; there are no bandages, no corn in the granary.

ENLIL: Ur will always claim my protection.

NIN-GAL: Your soldiers capture my messengers; they return to me with amputated noses.

ENLIL: Your messengers are ill mannered: they attribute pornographic messages to their Goddess.

NIN-GAL: They are my messages.

ENLIL: I will never believe it.

NIN-GAL: Your soldiers burn the crops, poison the waterways.

ENLIL: Fiction! See how the enemies of Sumer – the Elamites, treacherous Eastern tribe – seduce my own daughter into believing their fictions!

NIN-GAL: Father, Ur is innocent; its people are not armed.

ENLIL: I regret, but don't object.

NIN-GAL: The people of my city have been reduced to eating grass.

ENLIL: Not too hungry to write godless poems.

NIN-GAL: They write for the future days.

ENLIL: Does anybody still worship me in your city?

NIN-GAL: I don't discourage it.

ENLIL: Little slut!

NIN-GAL: Father, the cities of Sumer are sick. The priests and the Generals suck life out of the eyes of the unborn child. In your palace no news comes to you, the walls are too thick.

ENLIL: I had a daughter once; where is she now?

NIN-GAL: Here, at your feet, suppliant.

ENLIL: Rebel and suppliant?

NIN-GAL: I am no rebel, Father.

ENLIL: What shall we call you then?

NIN-GAL: I want to cleanse the lands of Sumer.

ENLIL: Char girl? Wash them in blood, char girl!

NIN-GAL: I want reform.

ENLIL: Daughter of the Gods: a reformer.

A long paper roll marked with cuneiform writing unrolls from above. DELITZCH enters and begins to decipher the writing.

NIN-GAL: I'm here with a request.

ENLIL: Ask.

NIN-GAL: Lift your siege.

ENLIL: Is that all?

NIN-GAL: That's all.

ENLIL: I, too, have a request.

NIN-GAL: Ask.

ENLIL: Bring me the head of your Elamite lover.

NIN-GAL: It is beautiful to me.

ENLIL: Bring me his little head.

NIN-GAL: It is precious to me.

ENLIL: I will hold it between my fingers like a bleeding snake.

NIN-GAL: Then Ur and its sisters will rise against you.

ENLIL: Force me into a slaughter I don't seek and call yourself a pacifist? What is this madness? What is this self loathing?

In deciphering the cuneiform script, DELITZCH pronounces ENKI's lines, in Sumerian.

ENKI/DELITZCH: Enlil, father of the Gods, the storm has been released.

NIN-GAL: Which storm?

ENKI/ DELITZCH: The storm decreed by the Council of the Gods.

NIN-GAL: Where is this storm?

ENLIL: See my chest: that is Sumer, Ur is its heart, everything that hurts Ur, hurts me here.

NIN-GAL: My city!

ENLIL: If you come to me again in pride, I will use you not like a daughter but like an unperfumed prostitute.

NIN-GAL: Nin-Gal has no father: Enlil has no daughter.

ENLIL exits.

SCENE 5: 1903 / 2015

DELITZCH, in a feverous state, touches NIN-GAL.

DELITZCH: Hands missing, eyeballs of shell and pupils of lapis lazuli.
Careful, Friedrich, don't slide along the walls, might lose yourself in a crack in the ruins...
Hunter amongst stones? Friedrich Delitzch!
Yes?
Shall you uncover honey, where maggots are?[8]

Enter KAISER WILHELM II, in a suit of armour.

DELITZCH: My Kaiser. My dear Father. I am a stray dog. Spit on me. *(Wraps his own eyes with a bandage like a hostage and goes down on his knees.)* Forgive me, forgive me.

KAISER WILHELM II: *(Through a loudspeaker, in Arabic.)* The destruction of images is never undertaken lightly. There is no hatred without true love. We know the real power

---

8   Charles Olson, *The Kingfishers*

of images. Today in the heretic West, Facebook removes
the idolatrous images of women's vaginas painted by men
like Gustave Corbet. Our message is convincing even
to the feminist ideologues. In the severing of a human
head, there is a meaning, a virtue, hard to discern at first.
Guardians of the false temples will learn it.

The KAISER executes DELITZCH.

SCENE 6: 2004 B.C.

PRIESTESS: *(Singing.)*
> Enlil called to the storm,
> The storm that annihilates the land,
> The evil storm that unpicks
> What was made,
> Like madness in the brain.

> The people groan.

> It howls above, it roars below.
> The wind, a rushing torrent,
> The evil wind smashes boats,
> Turns skulls into dropped eggs.
> Dark at its base, whip of rain in hand:
> It comes closer, the fires burn white.

> The people groan.

SCENE 7: 2004 B.C.

ELAM: Gas! Carried by the South wind: odourless, colourless.
They breath: throats strain, eyes bulge, legs writhe and life
leaps from open mouths. Bodies dash to the earth like fat
drops of rain on a dry summer path. The men will fight.

NIN-GAL: Ur has no time to waste on fighting.

ELAM: They've opened the armories, taken the weapons. They saw their dead babies, now they're hunting their killers.

NIN-GAL: Burn the armoury! Ur will have no more armory.

ELAM: While you dined at your father's palace-

NIN-GAL: Who said I dined?

ELAM: Ur was massacred!

NIN-GAL: Burn the armoury, I said. Where are my scribes?

ELAM: Sleeping.

NIN-GAL: Wake them!

ELAM: There's madness in your gaze.

NIN-GAL: I see over the horizon; what I see is terrible.

ELAM: Suspicion is rife, Ur no longer trusts you. The people are gathering outside the palace. Speak to them, before they rip your scribes limb from limb.

NIN-GAL: Extremity engenders its double.

ELAM: You are extremity, you are its double!

NIN-GAL: I'll address my people.

ELAM kisses NIN-GAL.

NIN-GAL: *(To DIYALA.)* Dress my neck. Only my neck.

ELAM: Let the drummers announce it: Nin-Gal will speak to Ur.

PRIESTESS: *(Singing.)*

>Desecrated planet. Executed sun.
>Dust piles high around the cups
>That held last night's wine;
>Nowhere to turn,
>The occupation occupies.
>Its agent's murder loudly in the square,
>Slay quiet in the alley,
>Those that thought to stay at home,
>Awake with slit throats.
>The storm sets up its central command,
>Lays the city in its grip, issues its decrees.
>The storm, the command of Enlil,
>Never resting, never ceasing,
>not even to catch breath
>from the orgies of blood:
>Covers Ur like a garment,
>Shrouds the streets like linen.

(Sound of camera shutters as at a Press Conference.)

You've seen the footage. There was a massacre, we know
that, but it remains unclear who the perpetrator was.
Investigations go on. We have no reason to believe Enlil
would be involved. We have no reason to believe Enlil
would not be involved. It's unclear. There are many
people out there. Everyone knows. There are Elamites,
for sure. There are facts, for sure. There are many facts.
There are as many facts as there are enemies, as there are
people. For sure. We just don't know. In the desert, red
lines are just not that red.

We condemn this massacre. It was a barbarous act. Our
sympathy goes out to the victims. An emergency relief

programme is being established. Tents are going up. If it gets worse, there will be action, a lot of action. I promise you that. The millions who suffer in one place will be re-housed in another. Perhaps in Europe. Perhaps next door. The dead will be mourned. We all care. Remember that.

Let's go through that footage again- in a more future way, you know?

(As lead singer in a band.) One, two, three, four!

(Repeats 'Desecrated Planet' as an anarcho-punk song.)

Act Four

SCENE 1: 2015

A large pack of dynamite is thrown onto the stage. The fuse burns momentarily, before extinguishing once. SOLDIER 1 enters to inspect the failure of this second device.

SOLDIER 1: Payload, big boy! You fucking supreme junk merchant, what are you? A right fucking beast of burden you are, Einstein, come here with your black hole and meet my fucking magic wand.

SCENE 2: 2004 B.C.

NIN-GAL: *(Naked.)* People of Ur, precious black-headed people of Ur, hear my dreams. I walked through a door into a valley blackened by fire. There, I saw a child crouched beneath a tree crying tears of blood, I opened my arms to the child who spat in my face and squawked; above us his mother, the vulture, circles the sun. Together they made a fire out of small bones.

I reached a temple with no incense where men genuflected, murmuring without singing. A group of them held a woman aloft and two men laid a saw between her legs and worked to cut her body into two, vagina first. Veiled priestesses with no eyes, sing: 'We cleanse our past, we prepare our future.' There, a young child holds the heart of a man to the sun, saying, 'This is my father's heart, my father was a traitor to God.' Veiled priestesses with no eyes , sing: 'We cleanse our past, we prepare our future.'

If this dream be true and if this be the future, will you say this is what Nin – Gal made? Nin-Gal who raises the walls of Ur high to the heavens and keeps the doors of the city open; Nin-Gal who frees the women of Sumer from bondage; Nin-Gal who inscribes her city's glory into the memory of the earth.

My father's soldiers have gone. Ur is without protection, within two turns of the sun, a second storm will be unleashed upon us, more evil and more deadly than the first: Ur will be an empty city, a dead city. Do not tremble at this knowledge: do not let your hearts sink with fear. There is nowhere to run. The Gods have turned against us and Ur is called upon to fight.

By dawn, my people, Ur needs one thousand poems for its scribes to pen. No sleep this night; we run to the future days, the coming days, the days that are not yet, they are our beloved children, they are our chambers, our gardens, our precious beads.

Let them say of Ur that it was a city that raised its walls to the sky but kept its doors open; a city that did not fight with weapons but instead wrote poems of exquisite beauty and even when death lowered upon it, Ur raised its face to the sun and impregnated into clay the horror that devours it.

Do not cry tyranny. What is to come is harder to bear.

What I dictate to you is the purest form of love.

SCENE 3: 2035

A dream sequence. The MAN, dressed as a surgeon, pushes in a replica of the WOMAN on an operating table. The WOMAN, dressed normally, enters holding a glass of wine. Music plays. The MAN opens a large incision in the replica's stomach, as the WOMAN giggles and groans in excitement. Out of the replica's stomach, the MAN draws a long metal stand followed by the multiple parts of a broken plaster bust. Medical assistants assemble the bust of NIN-GAL's head. The bust remains on stage until the end. The following verses, a free adaptation of stanzas from Rainer Marie Rilke's 'Das Solden Nachte', written by Iraqi performance poet Kathem Khanjar to accompany this scene, are sung in Iraqi Futurist Music style.

Night that looks the same in all cities,
Cities submerged in a sea of flags:
What do we do
With a small graveyard?

The cloud doesn't know the melting corpse
Hunched over the melted wheel
Sat in the melting chair;
Its taste
Lingers on the hand
For years.

SCENE 4: 2004 B.C.

NIN-GAL: Their poems are bad.

DIYALA: What do you expect?

NIN-GAL: Of the thousand I ordered, only ten are worth inscribing.

DIYALA: My son –

NIN-GAL: Is amongst them?

DIYALA: He can't feed his children.

NIN-GAL: Let him write better, I'll give him grain from my own rations.

DIYALA: His back is in tatters, his body in pain, his children –

NIN-GAL: Let him write better.

DIYALA: He can't!

NIN-GAL: The doors are open! Where will you go?

DIYALA: Return to your father, hide in a ditch.

NIN-GAL: And be whipped and spat upon?

DIYALA: Let us live, Nin-Gal.

NIN-GAL: Do you believe in me?

DIYALA: We worship you –

NIN-GAL: I didn't ask you about worship, I asked about your belief.

DIYALA: …

NIN-GAL: Death is near.

DIYALA: *(Speaking, for the first time.)* My son!

NIN-GAL: He must be whipped and his children go hungry. He has in him verses not uttered yet.

Drums in the distance. Enter ELAM.

ELAM: Their drums. They've come.

NIN-GAL: Who?

ELAM: The Elamite army.

NIN-GAL: Is that how Ur must end?

ELAM: Close the doors of Ur.

NIN-GAL: Never.

ELAM: You know what they will do. You've seen it. You've seen it in your dreams and you do nothing to prevent it. You abuse Ur to build Nin-Gal's glory.

NIN-GAL: How dare you?

ELAM: You. Only you. Endless vanity of you.

NIN-GAL: Show me your sex.

ELAM: You are no better than your Father.

NIN-GAL: Hard, you are the body of my resilience.
Limp, you are the body of my chosen death…
You are a traitor, Elamite!

ELAM: I never betrayed you.

NIN-GAL: Clap now, dance! Your people are invading my city!

ELAM: You've killed me.

NIN-GAL: Perhaps they'll crown you King of Ur!

ELAM: Where with this body now?

NIN-GAL: I don't care. You are dead.

Exit ELAM.

Write, scribes! Write until your eyes seize with cramps, until they cut your hands from the wrists, make clear marks in the wet clay for the future days, in the days to come the illiterates will roam the earth and words will be harder to decipher. Bring them light! Fill the kilns, lay the hot tablets in the burial chambers. They will kill every woman, every child, they will break everything they find, hide our secrets under the earth.

NIN-GAL, seized by the final vision, chants.

u-ama-nu-zu-ri	u-a-a-nu-zu-ri
u-am-nu-zu-ri	u-ses-nu-zu-ri
u-nin-nu-zu-ri	u-ses-nu-zu-ri
u-uku-nu-zu-ri	u-ma-gal-nu-zu-ri[9]

SCENE 5: 2004 B.C.

PRIESTESS: Is this a city or a broken ceramic?

The axe rises:
the people groan.

On its walls and high gates,
Where, before sunset, couples strolled
Is where they lie now, mouths agape.
In the market, where fruit and lettuce were piled,
In the halls, where dances and ribbons flowed,
Stacked high, now, corpse upon corpse.
Blood lubbers down pavements like molten bronze
And like pieces of fat on a hot plate,
Bodies melt into the earth's openings.

The people groan.

Struck down with no helmets, no loin cloths,
Bleeding with no bandages,

---

9 Lines 400–404 of 'The Lamentation for the Destruction of UR' translated by S.N. Kramer: 'The storm which knows not the mother, The storm which knows not the father, the storm which knows not the wife, the storm which knows not the child, the storm which knows not the brother, the storm which knows not the weak, the storm which knows not the strong, the storm on whose account the wife is forsaken, the storm on whose account the child is forsaken.'

Like a gazelle caught in a trap, its lips chapped in the dust;
Like drunkards their heads drooped on their necks;
The guards were killed,
The unarmed were killed with their backs turned,
The ones who stayed home, felt safe and were burned,
The strong and the frail died of hunger,
The mother ran from her child,
The father caste his eyes down
When the finger was pointed at his son:
The suckling child is gone, like big waters carry off a fish.

The people groan.

(Pointing at NIN-GAL.)

And above this city, like a mad bird,
She: the woman, the goddess, roams:
She abandoned this city.
Don't let her say she didn't,
She stood aside like an enemy.

The axe falls.
The people groan.

Act Five

The space is altered – by lighting – to feel like a lecture room. KHALED AL ASAAD, an older gentlemen, dressed in the pastel colours of a cotton Safari suit and wearing thick bifocal lenses, enters and smiles gracefully.

KHALED: Good evening. My name is Khaled Al Asaad, I come from Syria. I am an Assyriologist and it is my honour to be amongst you this evening to present you this brief overview of one of the most remarkable pieces of Sumerian literature available to us today, *The Lamentation for the Destruction of UR.*

Of the numerous Sumerian epics and myths, hymns and lamentations, proverbs and 'wisdom' texts that have come down to us on tablets dating from the early post-Sumerian period, the great majority are in such a state of incompleteness that, although large portions of the compositions can be pieced together from the various duplicating fragments, it is impossible to obtain a clear and satisfactory picture of their contents as a whole. For the serious translator of this material, this unfortunate fact amounts to a tragedy, for it robs him of an all-important element of control against slipping into a biased attitude in his interpretation of the individual passages.

The lament, as a genre, is one – I must confess – I have reservations over. It is one, that from the perspective of political history, is most disappointing because – for all its poetic bemoaning of the sorry plight of the Sumerian cities in times of misfortune and defeat – the lament pays, on the whole, little heed to the historical events which brought about this melancholy state of events and is therefore – literary considerations aside – *utterly devoid of interest.*

It is the 'why' that is lacking, and without the 'why', impossible to know where headlong we tumble, or even why we go.

He puts away his lecture notes, removes his glasses.

I am the martyr Khaled Al Asaad born January 1st 1932 died August 18th 2015. I spent my life protecting graves and now I'm looking for one for myself. A watery grave, a sandy grave, a European, Middle Eastern or African grave. A grave is a grave is a grave. The clay tablet is a tombstone for an entire city and my body – hung on a pole on the main road near the cultural centre in the Syrian town of Palmyra – my headless corpse, is the tombstone of other cities. I am the Aleppan, the Ninewan, the Homsian, the Mosuli, the Adani, the Gazan.

Make space, make space: the clay is not yet dry, the reed continues to scour.

SCENE 2: 1903

DELITZCH: In your notes from two months ago, you claim to have discovered a large chamber in sector fifty-seven, at nine metres under ground.

KOLDEWEY: Yes, we suspect it to be a banqueting hall.

ANDRAE: Or a sacrificial tomb?

DELITZCH: Twelve weeks ago.

KOLDEWEY: Correct.

DELITZCH: You have 200 Arabs employed on this dig?

ANDRAE: 250, actually.

DELITZCH: And why has this chamber not been opened?

KOLDEWEY: The walls are too thick.

DELITZCH: Perhaps my brain is too thick, say again?

KOLDEWEY: They are seven metres thick.

DELITZCH: A tunnel?

KOLDEWEY: Our resources are busy revealing the ramparts.

DELITZCH: Ramparts contain no texts, no words, no meanings.

KOLDEWEY: You received a crate of texts last month.

DELITZCH: Inconsequential lists!

KOLDEWEY: Two thousand tablets!

DELITZCH: Sheep and cattle deals!

KOLDEWEY: How was I supposed to know that?

DELITZCH: Your ignorance of Akkadian was never in doubt.

KOLDEWEY: My Akkadian is better than your Arabic.

DELITZCH: The German people have no need of dead cities! We need the roots of words, Sumerian words, dead words, yes! Out of the cuneiform wedges, I summon an army of dead words that liberates us from the idolatry of the Israelites!

ANDRAE: What of Holy Writ?

DELITZCH: Jews have no claim on it.

ANDRAE: What of the Old Testament?

DELITZCH: Irrelevant!

ANDRAE: I am a believer, Herr Delitzch, and a German.

DELITZCH: Prepare to cleanse your soul.

ANDRAE: I'm a man of God and the Holy Book.

DELITZCH: I too am a man of God.

ANDRAE: I read Genesis and feel awe.

DELITZCH: Read Gilgamesh and apprehend that here in Mesoptamia – not in Zion – lie the seeds of our Christian faith. Our German nation was conceived here.

KOLDEWEY: I see no blondes in Mesopotamia, Herr Delitzch.

DELITZCH: Take a better look at me.

ANDRAE: I will not be led into this slaughterhouse.

DELITZCH: *(To KOLDEWEY.)* Tomorrow morning you will eventrate the chamber in sector 57 –

ANDRAE: No!

DELITZCH: Or I will have you replaced!

KOLDEWEY: *(Conceding, to ANDRAE.)* Inform Hammoudi.

DELITZCH: Hammoudi has received his orders. I walk alone through Babylon like Nebuchadnezzar, 'lu-ti-bu-u lu-za-ak – tu…'

Exit DELITZCH.

ANDRAE: He wants to sap the life force from Christianity, extinguish the elixir!

KOLDEWEY: His project is darker than he knows.

ANDRAE: When you open the chamber, let me in first.

KOLDEWEY: What for?

ANDRAE: I will smash the inscriptions.

KOLDEWEY: What?

ANDRAE: Won't let that heretic son of Lutheran appropriate the meaning of those texts, I'll rent each word into a thousand fragments, dissolve his eyes in the puzzle!

KOLDEWEY: I love you.

ANDRAE: Delitzch seeks the spirit of Germania in the land of Nebuchadnezzar? *(ANDRAE takes a hammer.)* I will show him my spirit.

KOLDEWEY: Your will is strong.

ANDRAE: Colossal Dissonance! *(Smashes a tablet.)*

Enter NIN-GAL.

NIN-GAL: Now I will cry: 'Alas for my city, alas for my house'.

KOLDEWEY: A good, strong will!

NIN-GAL: Cursed, torn, broken, burnt.

ANDRAE: *(Smashing tablets.)* Insoluble disharmony!

NIN-GAL: My possessions, like a flock of rooks rising up, have left me.

KOLDEWEY: *(With sudden poise.)* Walter! The serpent dragon is not a mythical creature: Walter, it is real!

ANDRAE: *(Smashing.)* Maximum despair! Loud joy!

Enter HAMMOUDI.

NIN-GAL: Now I will cry 'O my possessions!'

HAMMOUDI: Herr Koldewey.

KOLDEWEY: What?

NIN-GAL: Men ignorant of silver fill their hands with silver,

HAMMOUDI: Al 7ujrah bil qata3 57. (The chamber in Sector 57.)

NIN-GAL: Men ignorant of gems fasten them around their neck.

KOLDEWEY: What of it?

HAMMOUDI: Fadhia. Mabyugah. (It's empty. Been looted.)

NIN-GAL: My small birds, nightingales, humming birds
Have flown away.

ANDRAE falls to his knees. KOLDEWEY's face is a mask of pain.

SCENE 3: (FOLLOW ON)

The BEETLE forms around NIN-GAL.

NIN-GAL: Now, I will say: 'Alas for my city!'

My girls are taken in boats
To wear strange emblems in strange lands,
My boys are hiding in a desert they do not know.

The city is no more.
Its people are dead.

In place of my city a strange city is being built.
What are these houses? Who are these people?
In place of my house a strange house is being built.

O my brickwork, o my house
Let me lie in your debris, curl up in your ruins;
Like the slaughtered ox, I will not rise.

I, the exile immigrant woman,
With the spittle of strange tribesmen on my face

The sting of foreign curses in my ears.

Words did not protect my city, it is no more.

I am its offerings, I am its walls, its brickwork:
I am all that is left.

Iridescent green, azure blue, veined turquoise:
beetle, my beetle, take the secrets back,
guard Ur's colours there, deep in the earth.

Enter the PRIESTESS. The BEETLE scatters.

I will not lower my head.
Write my crimes onto the stones of my stoning,
Stones more eloquent than you.

PRIESTESS: You are no longer Ur's Mistress
You are no longer Ur's lover.

The houses are toothless mouths,
The wells are bags of scorpions,
The classrooms are all empty,
Your gold, your statues, your carpets
Are taken to other lands.

You are no longer Ur's Mistress,
You are no longer Ur's lover

You watched this happen,
Music makes you weep,
Milk makes you weep,
Honey makes you weep,

You witnessed the execution of the sun,
And stood aside like an enemy,
And now your city is an orphan,
Your city is a beggar.

You are no longer Ur's Mistress
You are no longer Ur's lover.

Can you make your heart into water,
Fill your cursed womb with earth?

The lapidation commences. NIN-GAL is killed.

SCENE 4: 2035

Light reveals the plaster bust of NIN-GAL mounted on a stele. HUSBAND and WIFE are having sex. The woman disengages abruptly.

HUSBAND: What happened?!

WIFE: Nothing.

HUSBAND: What's the matter?

WIFE: I can't.

HUSBAND: Why not?

WIFE: *(Indicating the plaster bust of NIN-GAL.)* I don't want that in my house.

HUSBAND: Sorry?

WIFE: It's morbid.

HUSBAND: It's an antique.

WIFE: I don't care.

HUSBAND: It's a Sumerian stone head –

WIFE: It's violent.

HUSBAND: ...from the third millennia B.C..

WIFE: Send it back.

HUSBAND: I bought it on the black market.

WIFE: Get rid of it!

HUSBAND: It's heritage, not garbage!

WIFE: She is not free.

HUSBAND: What do you mean?

WIFE: I'm pregnant.

Pause.

HUSBAND: They'll kill us both.

SCENE 5: 2035

MUSEUM CURATOR: *(Singing.)*
    Nin-Gal is not dead,
    Nin-Gal cannot die,
    Never did Nin-Gal decree her vulva sacred,
    Never did an Elamite lay foot in her chamber:

    It was the storm, the sun-killing storm:
    May the gate of night be closed on the storm,
    Of its passage no record, no number, no index,
    May all its signifiers hang by a nail outside the door
    of creation:
    Drums, flutes, bodies proclaim her glory
    Now and into the future days.

SCENE 6: 2015

ISIS Soldiers work together frantically to stretch a roll of explosive wire across the length of the stage, above head height.

SOLDIER 2: Eins – Zwei – Drei!

The explosive wire is lit and burns across the stage.

END.

مسرحية مستوحاة من النص السومري لرثاء دمار مدينة أُوْر.

تأليف سليمان البسام

فيما يلي المشاهد من أُوْر 2004 قبل الميلاد، كما أنها مشاهد تحاكي الحرب الأهلية السورية في الفترة (2011-2015م).

الشخصيات:

إنليل:	أبو الآلهة، إله الريح- والد نين-غال
إنكي:	إله الماء- عم نين غال
نـانـا:	إله القمر واله مدينة أور- زوج نين-غال
نيـن_غـال:	آلهة القصب وملكة مدينة أور – زوجة نـانـا
الكاهنة:	كبيرة كهنة المعبد في أور
العيلامي:	عشيق نين-غال
ديـالا:	وصيفة نين-غال- خرساء*
خنفساء:	حاملة رؤى نين-غال

*تؤدي جملها بالإيحاء الجسدي

(أصوات مزامير وطبول النصر تأتي من خارج غرفة مظلمة)

نين-غال: رأيت كاحليه في السلاسل. ساقاهُ صلبتان كقوارب القصبِ، ركبتاهُ تلمعان كخُوَذٍ مصنوعةٍ من نحاسٍ، فخذاهُ يتصاعدان كالدخان من القفص.. وركبةُ ضفتا نهرٍ... بطنهُ كعرفِ الجملِ. صدرُهُ حقلٌ محروثٌ... كبتي؟

ديالى: كبتُ.

نين-غال: خصيتاهُ بلحٌ صلبٌ... قضيبُهُ دربٌ يؤدي لأبوابِ مدينةٍ جديدة، طيرُهُ غزالٌ إذا قفز... ظهرُهُ كظلِ شجرةِ أرزٍ... كتفاهُ مرصعةٌ بالفضةِ كالأبواب... عنقه يفرُ كمالكٍ حزينٍ إذا فزع... ذقنُهُ كالجلودِ المرصعة... شفتاهُ جدائل في حبلٍ جديد، وجراحه – ثلاثةُ جراحٍ- كلها مفتوحة...

ديالى: هذه غرفة مظلمة يا نين-غال.

نين-غال: ليست مظلمة.

ديالى: أفتح نافذة.

نين-غال: لا تفتحي نافذة.

ديالى: اسمعي المزامير، رجالنا عادوا... النصر لنا... زوجك ينتظرك يا نين-غال...

نين-غال: إخرسي أنتِ ونشوة نصركِ، تتذكرين الوصف؟

ديالى: أتذكره.

نين-غال: ستجدينه في السجن...

ديالى: هذه غرفة فتنة يا نين-غال. أفتح نافذة.

نين-غال: لن تفتحيها. إتلي عليه ما أقول.

ديالى: ماذا تقولين؟

نين-غال: قولي له: سيدتي تقول: "أيها العيلامي؛ عدو أور كاحلاكَ لم تُخلقا للسلاسلْ، كاحلاكَ خُلقا لركلِ الهواء المكدسِ في قاعدةِ سريري...".

(ديالى تهز رأسها)

نين-غال:

أعرف تماماً ما أريد... أريدُ أكثر مما أعرف.

الكاهنة:	(تنشد من الرُّقُم): " نين-غال ملكة أور تعلنُ ما يلي:

أولاً: أور مدينةٌ مفتوحة وبواباتها لن تُغلقَ أبداً.

ثانياً: أور تفتحُ ذراعيها لأي رجل، سومرياً كان أم عُبيداً أم أُكادياً أم عيلامياً شرط أن يرتلَ أشعاراً تستأهلُ الخلود على ألواح رُقُم أور، أو يغني أغنيةً تستحق التلحين، أو يخترع أداةً تقلل من كدح الإنسان.

ثالثاً: لأور سبعةُ أبواب، كلُ بابٍ هو بوابةُ رحمٍ للخصوبة، وللشعر الإباحي مقامٌ خاص، والأبيات التي تصف كمال النهدين، سر الزورق الرفيع، أو تحتفي باللعق وطقوس الجنس لها مكانةٌ خاصةٍ في أور.

رابعاً: نساء أور في حلٍّ من القيود الزوجية، حراتٌ بأن يتخذن لهن من الشارع عشاقاً دون أن يخشين حد الزنا، حراتٌ بمشاركة أجسادهن قبل وأثناء وبعد اتخاذ الأزواج.

خامساً: كهنة المعابد الزائفون، الكهنة الذين يعتدون على الأرامل، الذين يأخذون ضرائب مبالغ بها على دفن الموتى، الذين ينتهكون أعراض الأيتام يُسجنون أو يُنفون، وحصصهم من الضرائب تُحول إلى الكتبة..".

نـانـا:	كفى.
الكاهنة:	لم أفرغ بعد.
نـانـا:	لن أسمع أكثر.
الكاهنة:	زوجتك..
نـانـا:	لا تُسمها زوجتي.
الكاهنة:	ماذا تريدُ أن أُسمّيها.
نـانـا:	نين-غال آلهة القصب.
الكاهنة:	نين-غال آلهة القصب أصدرت هذا المرسوم، تسميه رؤيا.
نـانـا:	ليست رؤيا، إنها مجزرة.
الكاهنة:	قرأت رُقُماً من مئات.
نـانـا:	مئات المجازر.
الكاهنة:	كتبتها يكتبون ليل نهار، أفران الرُّقُم لا تبرد.
نـانـا:	كسّري الأفران.
الكاهنة:	خبأتها كلها تحت الأرض.

نانـا:	اقطعي أيادي الكتبة.
الكاهنة:	صرفت الجيش و وضعتُ الكتبة في الثكنات.
نانـا:	أنا إله هذي المدينة.
الكاهنة:	كل ليلةٍ ترسلُ رسلها، يُهَرِّبونَ أكياس الرُّقُمَ إلى مدن سومر الأخرى. تبث قوانينها المعتوهة وأشعارها الإباحية وأغانيها المجنونة في أرض سومر كلها.
نانـا:	أنا نـانـا.
الكاهنة:	الشعبُ هائمٌ بها، في أور يصلون لنين‑غال، في لاكاش يغنون لنين‑غال، في أكاد ينحتون تماثيل لمؤخرتها.
نانـا:	وهل لديها مؤخرة أصلاً؟
الكاهنة:	تدعي أن الخنفساء تأتيها بالرؤى.
نانـا:	أيُّ خنفساء؟
الكاهنة:	خفنساء زرقاء، أرجوانية، خضراء.
نانـا:	احرقي المدينة.
الكاهنة:	بناؤها استغرق خمسمائة عام.
نانـا:	أكتبي لأبيها إنليل، أبلغيه أن يرسل جنوده بفؤوسٍ مرفوعة..
الكاهنة:	تريده أن يهاجم ابنته؟
نانـا:	هي تهاجِمُه، تهاجِمُني، تهاجِمُ كل الآلهة.
الكاهنة:	ويفتَحُ أبواب الحرب الأهلية.
نانـا:	هذه حربٌ أهلية.
الكاهنة:	هي تتواصل مع "آخر".
نانـا:	تتواصل؟
الكاهنة:	تتواصل.
نانـا:	ما معنى تتواصل؟
الكاهنة:	تتواصل.
نانـا:	قصدك أنها تتناكح؟ تتناكح! تتناكح!
الكاهنة:	جنرال
نانـا:	جنرال ؟
الكاهنة:	أسير حرب
نانـا:	أسير حرب ؟
الكاهنة:	عيلامي

عيلامي؟	نـانـا:
عيلاميٌّ حرٌّ طليقٌ في أور؟ همجيٌّ يمارس نخولته داخل أسوار مدينتي؟ شاربُ دماء شعبي يقذف على أرضيات بلاطي؟	
أنقل لك ما تيقنت منه.	الكاهنة:
آتيني بها.	نـانـا:
ترفضُ رؤيتكَ.	الكاهنة:
أنتِ كاهنة.	نـانـا:
نعم.	الكاهنة:
تغنين رؤاها؟	نـانـا:
نعم.	الكاهنة:
كونيها.	نـانـا:
نعم؟	الكاهنة:
كونيها.	نـانـا:
أنا كاهنة.	الكاهنة:
(الكاهنة تفهم طلب نـانـا المبطن وتتقمص شخصية نين-غال)	
لقد تجاوزتِ كل مبادئ الحشمة يا نين-غال.	نـانـا:
حشمتُك كانت قيداً حول عنقي يا نانا.	الكاهنة:
انعدم الشرف؟ خرجتُ لأدافع عن أور، ائتمنك عليها، حولتِها إلى ماخور سومر.	نـانـا:
أخلق لأور مجداً في التاريخ.	الكاهنة:
بأن تحلي جيشها يا خرفة؟	نـانـا:
(يعبر العيلامي الخشبة ملطخاً بالدماء)	
أور لا تحتاج جيشاً.	الكاهنة:
(ساخراً) لا تبلغوا العيلاميين!	نـانـا:
كبّة، مسامير، ألواحٌ طينية، قصائد فائقة الجمال، أفرانٌ حامية. هذا هو جيش أور.	الكاهنة:
ما شاء الله، (مصححاً لنفسه) ما شاء نانا.	نـانـا:
تشكيلاته لا تعد ولا تحصى، جيش أور أكبر من أي جيش.	الكاهنة:
(مشيرة للعيلامي) هذا هو قائد جيشي. أنظر إلى جسده.. ينبت فيّ..	
بدعة.	نـانـا:

الكاهنة:	يتبرعم داخلي..
نـانـا:	ثورة.
الكاهنة:	يولج..
نـانـا:	قذارة.
الكاهنة:	..كولوج الخس!
نـانـا:	كفى، في زورق نين-غال الرفيع سأصبُ القُطران المغلي. بُصاق. خروج.

٣

العيلامي:	لا تتوقعي من أبناء شعبك أن يحتملوا.
نين- غال:	يحتملوا ماذا؟
العيلامي:	قناعاتكُ، مشروعكُ.
نين- غال:	قناعاتي لا تُحتمل، أحملها وحدي.
العيلامي:	بطئكُ ليست خاويةً كبطونهم.
نين- غال:	اللعنةُ على البطون، منذ متى تخلق البطون مجداً؟ ها هي بطني كتلة شحمٍ محترئة لا تحملها إلا أيادي عدو أبي. بطنُ عارٍ هي. ضع رأسك عليها أيها العيلامي.
العيلامي:	مجلسُ الآلهة سيتخلى عنك.
نين- غال:	طبعاً سيتخلون عني فأنا أريد مجلس بشرٍ لا آلهة.
العيلامي:	لن ترحمك.
نين- غال:	لا أخطب رحمتها.
العيلامي:	ماذا تخطبين؟
نين- غال:	أخطبك أنت.
	(تسمع نشيد الكاهنة) اسمع، إنهم يغنونها.
الكاهنة:	(تنشد مقطع من الزُّقُم) لقد هَجر اصطبله، وحظيرته قد أُسلمت للريح.
العيلامي:	رؤيا الليلة الفائتة؟
نين- غال:	نعم، سومر مريضة، وعاءٌ خاوٍ، جسدٌ عليل. اسمع.

الكاهنة:	<u>(تُنشد)</u>
	أيتها المدينة الميتة
	اسمكِ حيٌّ
	وأنت الميتة
	أسوارُكِ الشاهقة
	تُحصُنُ الموت
نين- غال:	أنتَ ترتجِف، بومضةِ عينٍ سيمحي كل هذا.
العيلامي:	لنرحلْ، لنفضِ بحبِنا إلى مكانٍ آخر.
نين- غال:	وهل حبُنا طفلٌ مريض؟
العيلامي:	لا ضرورةَ لـ...
نين- غال:	كلها ضرورةٌ قصوى.
العيلامي:	سأفرُ بكِ إلى الجبال، ستُسقيكِ يدايَ الماءَ من أنقى الينابيع.
نين- غال:	لا تخذلني برومنسيتك.
العيلامي:	أنا جنديٌّ يا نين- غال.
نين- غال:	بطلٌ أنت ولا شك.
العيلامي:	دعيني أسلح رجالَ أور، يريدون القتال دفاعاً عن مدينتهم.
نين- غال:	لو أردتُ الحربَ لما اتخذتُ من عدو شعبي عشيقاً في سريري.
العيلامي:	إذاً اقطعي رأسي واحمليه إلى أبيكِ وأطلبي غُفرانه.
نين- غال:	أيها العيلامي ذو العيون الشرسة، هل أصبحتَ ماعزَ قربان؟
العيلامي:	إذهبي إليه، حصارُه يخنق أور، لا دواء للعلاج، لا خبزَ في المخابز، ولا حتى سمكاً في الشِباك.
نين- غال:	في الماضي، حين كان أبناء فلاحي قرى أور يحلمون أن يكونوا كتبة، كان آباؤهم يذهبون بهم إلى كبار القوم الذين يأخذون مطرقةً كبيرة و ينهالون بها على أيدي الأطفال حتى تتقفع، وبهذا يُجنبون القريةَ خسارةَ فلاح.
	أبي أبو الآلهة إنليل استحسن هذا التقليد وكان يرسل لكبارِ القوم مطارق جديدة في نهايات مواسم الحصاد. مذ أصبحت ملكة أور أصبح أبناء القرى يتسابقون ليصبحوا كتبة وآباؤهم يعينوهم.
	يدُ الطفلِ بيدي، لن تبقى كذلك طويلاً، سيفصلونها، وقد تُخلعُ يدي من جذورها لكن ما دامت يدُ الطفلِ بيدي فسأعلمها نقش ما لن يُمحى، ما تنقشه أور لن يُمحى.

العيلامي:	كلماتي نداءُ توسلٍ وكلامي تضرُّع..
نين- غال:	لا تُطِل، اتّخذتُ قراري، سأزور أبي.
نين- غال:	أُنثرني، غمِّسْني بالزيت، فُضِّني، أبحرُ بزورقي الرفيع.
	إن استقمتَ فأنتَ درعُ جسدي.
	وإن خذلتني فأنت الموتُ الذي أنجبته خطيئتي.

٤

(أمام قصر إنليل)

ديالى:	و الآن؟
نين- غال:	أسوأ من قبل، لا تُفلتي يدي.
ديالى:	منذ ساعتين وأنتِ ضريرة. سأنادي الطبيب.
نين- غال:	لا حاجة للطبيب، الخنفساءُ لم تحسِمْ أمرَها بعد.
ديالى:	آفة.
نين- غال:	اخرسي!
ديالى:	جدرانُ هذا القصرِ باردة وأبوابه سميكة.
نين- غال:	إن مُتُّ فليقولوا عني أني رفعتُ أسوارَ أور حتى السماء وأبقيتُ أبوابَها مشرعةً ليل نهار
ديالى:	تتحدينَ الأقدارُ، العيلاميون يسلبون الريف، يرفعون الأطفالَ على أسنّةِ الرماح، و يحرقون الصيادينَ في الأقفاص، لولا جيشُ أبيك الذي يحتوينا بحصاره لابتلع البرابرة أور منذ أشهر.
نين- غال:	أنتِ لا تفهمين مدى قوةِ بابٍ مفتوح.
ديالى:	مولاتي، إنهم يخرجون من بلاط أبيك.
نين- غال:	لا أبصرُ شيئاً، صِفي لي ما ترين.
ديالى:	لا.
نين- غال:	أين ذهبتِ؟
ديالى:	لا أقوى على الوصف.
نين- غال:	بصري مشوش، صِفي لي ماذا هناك.

ديالى:	ما أراهُ هو الهلاك.
نين-غال:	صِفي لي.
ديالى:	العيلاميون أعداءُ سومر، و ملكهم عدو سومر مرفوعٌ على الأكتاف في بلاط أبيك، الجواهرُ تتلامعُ على صدره، أتباعُه يرفعون أقداحهم، يُغنّونَ ويَشتمونَ، والنبيذُ يطلُّ من لحاهم كالدم. آلهتنا استقبلت أعدائنا ولبت مطالبهم، هذا نذيرُ شؤم وأخشى ما أخشاه.
نين-غال:	العمى نعمة.. أتَثُ!
	(استولت عليها رؤيا)
الكاهنة:	*(تنشد)* أنا كالطير المحلّقُ فوق المدينة المدمرة.
	"أور" تحتي بدمائها ملطخة.
	تخترق العاصفةُ المدينة
	كما تخترق أصابع اليد القفاز.
	أصرخُ: عودي إلى صحرائك أيتها العاصفة.
	لكن العاصفة لا ترضخ.
ديالى:	أبوكِ يومي لك، أدخلي عليه.

٥

نين-غال:	هم في أماكنهم ثابتون وأنا أقترب منهم. الماء في جرارٍ المرمر ساكن. ينسكب زمناً.
إنليل:	ابتسمي لك يا حبيبتي، إعلمي أن قلبي قلب أبٍ ملئٍ بالحنان. اقتربي، قبّلي رأس أبيكِ يا أبنتي الحبيبةُ المقدسة.
نين-غال:	أبي، وضعتَ مدينتي أور تحت حصارٍ أليم.
إنليل:	أبداً، وضعتُ أور تحت حمايتي.
نين-غال:	هذا الشهر الثالث، نفذ الضماد والمخازن خلت من القمح والذرة.
إنليل:	أور عزيزةٌ على قلبي، سأحميها إلى الأبد.
نين-غال:	جنودكَ يقتلون رسلي ويعيدونهم إليَّ مجدوعي الأنوف.
إنليل:	رُسلكِ كاذبون، ينسبون لكِ ما يحملون من إباحيات.
نين-غال:	هم يحملون رسائلي.

إنليل:	لن أصدق هذا أبداً.
نين-خال:	جُنودكَ يحرقون الحقول، يُسممون السواقي.
إنليل:	أقاويل، أرأيتِ كيف أن أعداء سومر، العيلاميون الهمج القادمين من الشرق يستدرجون حتى ابنتي لتصديق رواياتهم.
نين-خال:	أبي، أور مدينة عُزَّلْ، شعبُها لا يحملُ السلاح.
إنليل:	مع الأسف، لكني لن أعارض هذا.
نين-خال:	الجوعُ دفع بشعبي إلى أكلِ العُشب.
إنليل:	الجوعى لا يكتبون الأشعار الكافرة.
نين-خال:	يكتبون للأيام المستقبلية.
إنليل:	هل بقي هناك من يعبدني في أور؟
نين-خال:	لم أمنعهم من عبادتك.
إنليل:	ساقطة، دنيئة.
نين-خال:	أبي، مدن سومر مريضة، الكهنة والجنرالات يمتصون الحياة حتى من أجنة الأرحام، وأنت لا ترى، لا تصل لك أنباء ما يحدث، جدرانك باردة وأبوابك سميكة.
إنليل:	كان لدي إبنة، أين هي الآن؟
نين-خال:	راكعةٌ عند قدميك.
إنليل:	متمردةٌ و راجية؟!
نين-خال:	لست متمردة يا أبي.
إنليل:	ماذا أسميك إذاً؟
نين-خال:	أتيتك بطلب.
إنليل:	أطلبي.
نين-خال:	أن ترفع حصارك عن أور.
إنليل:	فقط؟
نين-خال:	فقط.
إنليل:	تم. وبالمقابل لي عندك طلب.
نين-خال:	قُلْ.
إنليل:	آتيني برأسِ عشيقك العيلامي.
نين-خال:	هو أغلى الرؤوس عندي.
إنليل:	آتيني برأسِه الصغير.

نين-غال: هو أثمن الرؤوس عندي.

إنليل: سأمسك به بين أصابعي كأفعى مقطوعة الرأس.

نين-غال: ستثور ضدك أور وشقيقاتها.

إنليل: أتهددِيني بأخواتِ أور؟ تدفعِيني إلى قتلٍ لا أريدهُ وتدعِينَ أنك مسالمة؟ ما هذا الجنون؟ ما كرهُ الذات هذا؟

(يدخل إنكي)

إنكي: أخي إنليل أبو الآلهة، العاصفة انطلقت.

نين-غال: أيةُ عاصفة؟

إنكي: العاصفة التي أقرها مجلس الآلهة.

نين-غال: أين تلك العاصفة؟

إنكي: أنظري إلى صدري، هذه سومر، أور قلبها، كل ما يؤلم أور ها هنا.

نين-غال: مدينتي !

إنليل: إن آتيتِ بغرورك هذا مرةً أخرى لن أتعامل معك كآبنة بل كأمرةٍ نتنة.

نين-غال: نين-غال يتيمةٌ لا أب لها وإنليل ليس لديه إبنة.

٦

الكاهنة: *(تنشد)* دعا "إنليل" العاصفة.
العاصفة التي تهتك الديار.
العاصفةُ الحقودة التي تمحو
كل ما قد كان.
مثل عقلٍ مسهُ الجنون.
الناس ينوحون.
العاصفةُ تعوي في السماء وتزأر في الأرض.
العاصفةُ كالطوفان.
تهجم العاصفة الحقودةُ على البلاد.
تُدمّر الزوارق كعملاقٍ يلهو.
تشطرُ الجماجمَ كفأس.
تحملُ المطرَ سوطاً في يدها.
عند اقترابها، نيرانُها تسعرُ الأحياء.
والناس ينوحون.

العيلامي:	غازٌ أتت به ريحُ الجنوب، دون رائحة، دون لون، تنفسوه: حناجرُهمْ تتشنج، عيونُهم تجحظ، أقدامهم تُشل والحياة تخرج من أفواههم زبداً. الأجساد ترتطم بالأرض كقطرات المطر في موسمِ الصيف. رجالُ أور سيقاتلون.
نين-غال:	لا وقت لدى أور تهدره على القتال.
العيلامي:	فتحوا ترسانةَ السلاح، أخذوا أسلحتَهم، رأوا أولادهم قتلى وهم الآن يبحثون عن القتلة.
نين-غال:	احرق الترسانة، أور لن يكون لديها ترسانة.
العيلامي:	بينما كنتِ هناك، تتناولين العشاء في قصر أبيك..
نين-غال:	من قال لك أنني تناولت العشاء...
العيلامي:	.. أور شهدت المجزرة.
نين-غال:	احرق الترسانة قلتُ لك..
العيلامي:	الجنون في عينيك.
نين-غال:	أرى ما وراء الأفق، وما أراه رهيب.
العيلامي:	فقدتِ ثقة أور. الحشود على أبواب بلاطك، خاطبي شعبَكِ قبل أن يمزقوا كتبتك.
نين-غال:	التطرف يولّدُ قرينه.
العيلامي:	أنتِ التطرفُ! وأنت قرينه! *(يقبلها العيلامي على فمها مطولاً)*
نين-غال:	سأخاطب شعبي. *(السدالى)* لتُبئى عنقي، عنقي فقط.
العيلامي:	فلتعلنها الطبول، نين-غال ستخاطب أور.

الكاهنة:	*(تنشد)*

أُغتُصِب الكوكب وأُعدِمَت الشمس.
لا هروب من غزوها.
عملاؤها يَذبحَون في الميادين.
عملاؤها يَقتلون في الأزقة.

ومن لزم دارهُ أُستُبيحَ دمهُ أمام ذويه.

العاصفة الحقودة.

فَرَضَت على المدينة شريعتها.

حاصرتُ المدينة.

أبادتُ المدينة.

بلا راحةٍ ولا كلل.

العاصفةُ التي أمر بها "إنليل"

غطّت "أور" كغباءة.

كَثّنَت حاراتها شارعاً شارعاً.

(صوت فلاشات كاميرا)

الكاهنة: (مخاطبةً الجمهور) شاهدتم الشريط.. مجزرة بلا شك، نعلم هذا... لكن الغموض مستمر حول من ارتكبها. التحريات مستمرة .. لا يوجد ما يستدعي الظن أن لإنليل يدٌ في الأمر... لا يوجد ما يستدعي الظن أنْ ليس لإنليل يدٌ في الأمر... الأمر غامض... هناك الكثيرون يضمرون لنا الشر... الكل يعرف... هناك عيلاميون، أكيد... هناك حقائق، أكيد... حقائق كثيرة، أكيد... حقائق بكثرة الأعداء وبكثرة الكثيرين، أكيد... حقيقة الأمر أننا لا نعرف... في الصحراء الخطوط الحمر... باهتة...

ندين المجزرة... فعلٌ همجي... قلوبنا مع الضحايا الأبرياء... تم وضع برنامج إسعاف وطوارئ... بدأنا بنصب الخيام... إذا تدهور الأمر سترون أكشِن... كثيرٌ من الأكشِن.. نعدكم بذلك...

الملايين الذين يعانون في مكان سيُنقلون إلى مكانٍ آخر... من هنا لهناك... ربما أوروبا... ربما الجوار... الموتى سيُرثّون ... قلبنا واحد... تذكروا... تفكروا... كلنا مخثون...

لنعد الشريط

In a more future way, you know

1,2,3,4

(تغني " أغتَصِبَ الكوكب" مرة أخرى بشكلٍ ماجن)

نين-خال: يا شعب أور

يا أصحاب الرؤوس السود الثمينة

اصغوا لرؤاي

فتحتُ باباً ودخلت وادياً عصفته النيران

رأيت طفلاً يجلس القرفصاء تحت شجرة

يبكي دموعاً من دم

فتحت له ذراعي

فبصق في وجهي ونعق

فوق رأسه تحت الشمس كانت تحوم أمه العقاب

معاً صنعا ناراً من عظام صغيرة

وعلى امتداد الوادي كانت النار تتكرر على ألواح الرُقُم الرطبة

وصلتُ إلى معبد خالٍ من البخور

ورأيت الرجال راكعين يثمثمون ولا يغنون

رفع جمعٌ منهم أنثى إلى السماوات

وأخذ إثنان منشاراً وضعوه بين ساقيها

كانوا يلهثون وهم يحاولون شطر جسدها نصفين

كاهناتٌ منقباتٌ ممحية عيونهن ينشدن:

نطهر ماضينا تحضيراً لمستقبلنا

وهناك طفلٌ أمسك بقلب رجل

رفعه نحو الشمس قائلاً: هذا قلب أبي الذي خان الله

كاهناتٌ منقباتٌ ممحية عيونهن ينشدن:

نطهر ماضينا تحضيراً لمستقبلنا

إن كان حلمي رؤية وإن كان هذا مستقبلنا

فهل ستقولون: هذا ما جنته نين-غال

نين-غال التي ترفع أسوار أور للسماوات وتبقي أبوابها مشرعة

نين-غال التي تحرر نساء سومر من عبوديتهن

نين-غال التي تنقش مجد أور في ذاكرة الأرض

أقول لكم الآن:

ما تزرعه أور اليوم سيُحصد غداً

ما تزرعه سومر اليوم سيُحصد غداً

جيش إنليل، الذي كان أبي، ضرب وهرب

تركنا لقدرنا

أور بدون حماية، خلال دورتي شمس عاصفةٌ أخرى ستجتاحنا، ستكون أكثر

شراسة وتدميراً من الأولى

أور ستكون مدينةً ميتة

لا ترتجفوا أمام هذا

لا تدعوا قلوبكم تغرق في الخوف

لا مفر

الآلهة انقلبت ضدنا وعلى أور أن تقاوم

قبل الفجر يا شعبي، أور تريد منكم ألف قصيدةٍ ينقشها الكتبة

لا نوم هذي الليلة

نفرُّ إلى الأيام القادمة، الأيام المستقبلية

الأيام التي لم تُنطق بعد

هي أبناؤنا، هي بيوتنا، هي حدائقنا، هي كنوزنا

فليقولوا عن أور أنها رفعت رأسها للسماوات

شيدت أسوارها الشاهقة وتركت أبوابها مشرعة

لم تقاتل بالسلاح، قاتلت بالأشعار فائقة الجمال

وحتى حين أتاها الموت رفعت رأسها للشمس

ونقشت على الرُقُم جمالاً يخلع فاجعة الموت

لا تتهموني بالطغيان، فالآتي أعظم.

وما أمليه عليكم أنقى أشكال الحُبّ.

أشعارهم رديئة.	**نين-غال:**
وماذا تتوقعين؟	**ديالى:**
من بين ألف قصيدةٍ أمرت بها، عشرةٌ فقط تستحق تخليدها على الرُقُم.	**نين-غال:**
ابني..	**ديالى:**
بينهم؟	**نين-غال:**
لا يستطيع إطعام أبنائه.	**ديالى:**
فليكتب شعراً أجمل وسأعطيه من طبقي.	**نين-غال:**
ظهره متفسخ، جسده منهك، أطفاله..	**ديالى:**
فليكتب شعراً أجمل.	**نين-غال:**
لا يستطيع.	**ديالى:**
الأبوابُ مفتوحة، أين ستذهبون؟	**نين-غال:**
نرجعُ لأبيك، نختبئ في أي حفرة.	**ديالى:**
لتهانوا و يُبصقُ عليكم في شتات المنافي؟!	**نين-غال:**
دعينا نعيش يا نين-غال.	**ديالى:**
هل تؤمنين بي؟	**نين-غال:**
نعبدك.	**ديالى:**
لم أسألكِ عن عبادتك بل عن إيمانك.	**نين-غال:**
...	**ديالى:**
الموتُ قريب.	**نين-غال:**
(تنطق) ابني.	**ديالى:**
عليه أن يُجلد وعلى ابنائه أن يجوعوا. لديه شعرٌ لم ينشده بعد.	**نين-غال:**
هذي طبولهم. وصلوا.	**العيلامي:**
من؟	**نين-غال:**
العيلاميون.	**العيلامي:**
أهذي نهاية أور إذاً؟	**نين-غال:**
أغلقي أبواب أور.	**العيلامي:**
أبداً.	**نين-غال:**
تعلمين ماذا سيفعلون، رأيتِه في رؤاكِ ولا تفعلين شيئاً لإيقافه.	**العيلامي:**

نين-خال:	أوتجرؤ؟
العيلامي:	أنتِ، أنتِ وفقط، غرورٌ لا حدود له.
نين-خال:	أريني لحولتك.
العيلامي:	لستِ أفضلَ من أبيك.
نين-خال:	إن استقمتَ فأنتَ درعُ جسدي، وإن خذلتني فأنت الموتُ الذي أنجبته خطيئتي. أنت خائنٌ يا عيلامي!
العيلامي:	لم أخنك يوماً.
نين-خال:	صفّق، ارقص، جيشك يغزو مدينتي.
العيلامي:	قتلتِني.
نين-خال:	من يدري ربما ينصبونك ملكاً على أور.
العيلامي:	أين أواري هذا الجسد الآن؟
نين-خال:	لا يهم، أنت ميت.
نين-خال:	انقشوا أيها الكتبة حتى تتجمد عيونكم، أكتبوا حتى يقطعوا أيديكم من المعصمين، في الأيام المستقبلية أميةٌ قاتلة، آتوهم بالنور، إملأوا الأفران. إخفوا الرُقُمَ في المدافن، ضعوها هناك ولا تنتظروا أن تبرد. سيقتلوا كل إمرأة، كل طفل، سوف يدمرون كل ما تصل إليه أيديهم. إخفوا عظمةُ أور تحت الأرض.

(تنشد)

أو آ آ نو زو ري	أو آما نو زو ري
أو شيش نو زو ري	أو آم نو زو ري
أو شيش أو زو ري	أو نين نو زو ري
أو ما قال نو زو ري*	أو أوكو نو زو ري

---

* الأسطر ٤٠٠-٤٠٤ من "رثاء مدينة أور".

الكاهنة: (تنشد)

أهذو مدينة

أم شظايا من فخّار.

يرتفع الفأس.

الناس ينوحون.

الجدران المتينة تهاوت.

والناس ينوحون.

عند البوابات العالية وفي الطرقات

تكدّست الجثث.

وفي حاراتها العريضة التي شهدت الاحتفالات

اختلط الموتى.

وذابت الأجساد من تلقاء نفسها.

مثل زبدةٍ تحت الشمس.

الناس ينوحون.

مطروحون على الأرض.

بلا أغطيةٍ على رؤوسهم.

كالغزلان في الفخ.

شفاههم يمزّغها التراب.

تتدلى رؤوسهم على أعناقهم كالسكارى.

الذين تمسكوا بسلاحهم أبيدوا.

والذين حاولوا الهرب أبيدوا.

وكالأجنة حين الولادة هم في دمائهم يصرخون.

هلَكَ القوي والضعيف من الجوع.

تركت الأمهات بناتهن.

ترك الآباء أبناءهم.

والصغار الذين لزموا أحضان أمهاتهم.

جرفهم الطوفان مثل السمك.

الناس ينوحون.
(مشيرةً إلى نين ـخال)
وآلهتهم سيدتهم.
مثل عصفور مجنون.
تلك الأنثى فوق مدينتها تحوم.
هَجَرَتْ مدينتها.
لا تسمحوا لها أن تنكر.
وقفت جانباً كالعدو.
.. ينزلُ الفأس
والناس ينوحون

خالد الأسعد: مساء الخير. اسمي خالد. لقد جئتُ من سوريا. أنا مختص بالآشوريات، ويشرفني أن أكُون بينكم هذا المساء لنقدم لكم هذه النبذة المختصرة لواحدة من أبرز القطع الأدبية السومرية المتاحة لنا اليوم، "رثاء مدينة أور". من بين الملاحم والأساطير السومرية العديدة، والأناشيد والنبوءات والأمثال ونصوص "الحكمة" التي وصلتنا على رُقُم تعود إلى الفترة المبكرة ما بعد السومرية، الغالبية العظمى منها في حالة عدم اكتمال، رغم أن أجزاءً كبيرة من الأغاني يمكن تجميعها معاً من مختلف الشظايا المستنسخة والمتكررة، فمن المستحيل الحصول على صورة واضحة ومُرضية لمحتوياتها كافة. بالنسبة للمترجم الخطير لهذه المادة، فإن هذه الحقيقة المؤسفة ترقى إلى المأساة، لأنها تسرق منه عنصراً هاماً من عناصر السيطرة ضد الانزلاق إلى موقف متحيز في تفسيره للمقاطع الفردية.

الرثاء، كنوع أدبي، هو واحد ـويجب أن أعترف أن لدي تحفظات كثيرة. إحداها أنه من منظور التاريخ السياسي، هي مخيبة للآمال أكثر، لأنه بالرغم من كل شعاعها الشاعري من المحنة المؤسفة للمدن السومرية في أوقات المحنة والهزيمة ـ فإن الرثاء يدفع، إجمالاً، قليلاً من الانتباه إلى الأحداث التاريخية التي أدت إلى هذه الأحداث الحزينة، وبالتالي فإن الاعتبارات الأدبية تخلو

من الاهتمام.

إنه "السبب" الذي يفتقر إليه، وبدون "السبب"، من المستحيل أن نعرف أين تعثّرنا، أو حتى لماذا نمضي.

(يضع مذكرات المحاضرة، ويزيل نظارته. قرع جرس في المسافة، الأنوار تتلاشى ببطء إلى اللون الأسود طوال مدة قراءة وصيته).

أنا الشهيد خالد الأسعد، مولود في أول كانون الثاني/ يناير 1932 ، مُتوفى في 18 آب/ أغسطس 2015. أفنيت عمري في البحث وفي حماية القبور. أنا الآن باحثٌ عن قبرٍ لي. قبرٌ رطب أو جاف لا فرق. قبر أوربي أو شرق أوسطي أو أفريقي لا فرق. في الموت تتساوى القبور. الرُقُمُ شاهدُ قبرٍ لمدينة. أنا الآن مقطوع الرأس، معلقٌ بمسمار في الشارع العام على بعد خطوات من المركز الثقافي في تدمر. جثةٌ يابسة. أنا الآن شاهدُ قبرٍ لمدنٍ أخرى؛ أنا حلبي، نينوي، حمصي، تدمري، موصلي، بنغازي، يمني. وسّعوا الساحة، وسّعوا الساحة، وسّعوا الساحة فالطين لا يزال رطباً والقلم مستمرٌ في النقش.

١٣

نين- غال: أريد أن أصرخ:
"آو يا مدينتي! آو يا بيتي! "
لُعنتِ، دُمِرتِ، كُسِّرتِ، أحرِقتِ
ممتلكاتي خطفها رفُّ الغربان
أريدُ أن أصرخ: " آو يا ممتلكاتي"
رجالٌ يجهلون قيمة الفضة ملأوا بها أيديهم.
وزيّنوا بها أعناقهم.
عصافيري الصغيرة، عنادلي، وكراويني فرت من أقفاصها.

(نين-غال تقود الخنفساء)

أريد أن أصرخ: "آو يا أور!"
بناتي سُبِينَ بزوارق أجنبية

ليلبسن شعارات غريبة في مدنٍ باردة
أبنائي يختبأون في صحاريَ مجهولة.

المدينة لم تعد مدينة
أُبيدَ شعبها.

في مكان مدينتي تُبنى مدينةٌ غريبة
ما هذه البيوت؟ من هم هؤلاء؟
في مكان بيتي يُبنى بيتٌ غريب.

يا جدران أور، يا بيتي
لأتمدد بين ركامك الدافئ
مثل الثور المذبوح، لن أنسلخ عنها

أنا المنفية، المهاجرة الملطخة بالعار
يُمَرَغُ وجهي ببصاق القبائل المعادية
ولعناتٌ تُنطقُ بلغةٍ لا أجيدها تملء أذناي:

الكلمات لم تحم مدينتي، مدينتي لم تعد مدينة
أنا قربناها، أنا أسوارها، أنا طوبها
أنا كل ما تبقى منها.

(للخنفساء) أخضرٌ قزحي، أزرقٌ فيروزي، تركوازي، أرجواني معرّقٌ،
استرجعي ألوانك أيتها الخنفساء، يا خنفسائي؛ احفظي أسرار أور، إخفي
ألوان أور عميقاً تحت الأرض.

لن أطأطئ رأسي
انقشوا جرائمي على الحجر الأصم. الأفصح منكم.

(يتم رجم نين-غال بشكل طقسي بالحجارة)

الكاهنة:

(تُنشد)

لم تعودي خطيبة أور، لم تعودي عشيقة أور

البيوت أفواهٍ خُلِعَتْ أسنانها

الآبار سُمِمت، البحيرات رُدِمتْ

فصول المدارس المهجورة تردد أناشيد أشباح المعذبين

في الشوارع حيث كانت الورود تنتشر الآن نعال الموتى

ذهبك وتماثيلك وبساطك الثمين يتاجر بها عبر الحدود كهنات الهوى

لم تعودي خطيبة أور، لم تعودي عشيقة أور

وقتِي مشاهدة

الأغاني تُبكيكِ

الحليب تُبكيكِ

العسل يُبكيكِ

شاهدتي إعدام الشمس

وقفتي جانباً كالعدو

مدينتك كمتسولٍ أصابته الشيخوخة

لم تعودي خطيبة أور، لم تعودي عشيقة أور

أبوسعك أن تحوّلي قلبك إلى ماء؟!

أبوسعك أن تردّي رحمك المنبوذ؟!

(نين-غال تموت)

الكاهنة: *(تنشد)*

نين-غال لم تمت.

نين-غال لا يمكنها أن تموت.

لم تُصدر مرسوماً بقداسة زورقها الرفيع.

ولم يدخل العيلامي حجرتها قط.

كانت العاصفة قاتلة الشمس.

فليغلق على العاصفة بابُ الليل الكبير.

لوجودها لا سجلٌ ولا رُقُمٌ ولا رُقُم.

فلتعلق جميع دلائلها على مسمارٍ خارج باب المعرفة.

إقرعوا الطبول، اعزفوا المزامير.

اعلنوا مجدها الآن وفي الأيام المستقبلية.

الطبول ، المزامير ، الأجساد تعلن مجدها.

الآن وفي الأيام المستقبلية.

تم

By the same author

Kalila wa Dimna
The Mirror for Princes
9781840026702

Petrol Station
9781786821492

WWW.OBERONBOOKS.COM

Follow us on Twitter @oberonbooks
& Facebook @OberonBooksLondon